# CULTURE SHOCK!

## A Survival Guide to Customs and Etiquette

# SINGAPORE

**Kelly Jackson-Nash**

**Marshall Cavendish**
Editions

Reprinted 2017

First published in 2006 and reprinted 2007, 2nd edition published in 2009 by Marshall Cavendish International (Asia) Private Limited; 3rd edition published in 2012 and reprinted 2013 and 2015 by Marshall Cavendish Corporation.

This 4th edition published by Marshall Cavendish Editions
An imprint of Marshall Cavendish International

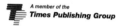

A member of the
**Times Publishing Group**

Other Marshall Cavendish Offices:
Marshall Cavendish Corporation. 99 White Plains Road, Tarrytown NY 10591-9001, USA • Marshall Cavendish International (Thailand) Co Ltd. 253 Asoke, 12th Flr, Sukhumvit 21 Road, Klongtoey Nua, Wattana, Bangkok 10110, Thailand • Marshall Cavendish (Malaysia) Sdn Bhd, Times Subang, Lot 46, Subang Hi-Tech Industrial Park, Batu Tiga, 40000 Shah Alam, Selangor Darul Ehsan, Malaysia

Marshall Cavendish is a registered trademark of Times Publishing Limited

**National Library Board, Singapore Cataloguing-in-Publication Data**

Name(s): Jackson-Nash, Kelly.
Title: CultureShock!. Singapore : a survival guide to customs and etiquette / Kelly Jackson-Nash.
Description: 4th edition. | Singapore : Marshall Cavendish Editions, [2016] | Series: Culture shock! | Includes index.
Identifier(s): OCN 950878967 | ISBN 978-981-4677-11-0 (paperback)
Subject(s): LCSH: Singapore--Social life and customs. | Etiquette--Singapore.
Classification: DDC 959.57--dc23

Printed in Singapore by Markono Print Media Pte Ltd

Photo Credits:
All photos by the author except for 'Malay couple' on page 73 by Ramlah Anwar
• Cover photo by the author

All illustrations by TRIGG

# ABOUT THE SERIES

Culture shock is a state of disorientation that can come over anyone who has been thrust into unknown surroundings, away from one's comfort zone. *CultureShock!* is a series of trusted and reputed guides which has, for decades, been helping expatriates and long-term visitors to cushion the impact of culture shock whenever they move to a new country.

Written by people who have lived in the country and experienced culture shock themselves, the authors share all the information necessary for anyone to cope with these feelings of disorientation more effectively. The guides are written in a style that is easy to read and covers a range of topics that will arm readers with enough advice, hints and tips to make their lives as normal as possible again.

Each book is structured in the same manner. It begins with the first impressions that visitors will have of that city or country. To understand a culture, one must first understand the people—where they came from, who they are, the values and traditions they live by, as well as their customs and etiquette. This is covered in the first half of the book.

Then on with the practical aspects—how to settle in with the greatest of ease. Authors walk readers through how to find accommodation, get the utilities and telecommunications up and running, enrol the children in school and keep in the pink of health. But that's not all. Once the essentials are out of the way, venture out and try the food, enjoy more of the culture and travel to other areas. Then be immersed in the language of the country before discovering more about the business side of things.

To round off, snippets of information are offered before readers are 'tested' on customs and etiquette. Useful words and phrases, a comprehensive resource guide and list of books for further research are also included for easy reference.

# CONTENTS

# ACKNOWLEDGEMENTS

It seems it takes a village to write a book.....

My thanks must first and foremost go to Justin Lau, Rachel Heng, Melvin Neo and everyone at Marshall Cavendish for this amazing opportunity. Thank you for your advice, reassurance, and guidance along the way. Apologies for the random apostrophes, missing words, and overly long sentences.

A big thank you to all of the people who knowingly (and unknowingly) have contributed to the writing of this book. I doubt there is a person I've encountered in Singapore this past year who hasn't helped in some way, even though they might not have even known!

The greatest pleasure in writing this book was the opportunity to learn more about Singapore and Singaporeans. I am eternally grateful to the Singaporeans who gave so freely and graciously of their time and knowledge, and never resented my 'just one more question!' emails. Rosalind Ong, Eisen Teo, Elisa Chia, Precious Marimuthu, Siti Mariam Binte Abu Bakar, Muru Pillay, Karen Lee, and Manisah Shariff—I couldn't have done this without you!

Heartfelt thanks to my family and friends who encouraged and supported me throughout this process. Extra special thanks to the four friends—Kirsten, Jen, Nora and JoDee— who talked me into saying "yes" to the book and saving me from a lifetime of regret!

Last, but not least, to my fellow expat adventurers—Mark, Caitlin and Hayley—for your love and support. I love you 96 million thousand and six. Ditto.

# DEDICATION

*For Caitlin and Hayley —*
*my inspirations*

# INTRODUCTION

If you're reading this book then you are either living in Singapore already or considering living in Singapore, or you know me (Hi Mum! Hi Dad!). So, let me make it apparent early in this book that I think living in Singapore is an amazing experience. Although every city and country in the world has its pros and cons, the dangers that come with many other locations are minimised in Singapore. As a mother, this gave me great comfort and assurance both before and after we relocated to Singapore.

We had already committed to moving to Singapore when I paid my first visit in 2010 on a stopover on the way home from Europe. Alone with my two daughters, I was taken ill in the middle of the night. With the help of some wonderful hotel staff and an incredibly efficient (and affordable!) hospital emergency department, both my daughters and I were incredibly well looked after. I knew from that experience that living in Singapore was an adventure that I wanted to take.

What people know about a particular country depends very much on where and when they grew up. For Australians like me, Singapore has had a relatively prominent place in our culture, partly due to the horrors of World War II and partly because of Singapore's handy location as a stopover destination on our way to other places. Whilst most Australians aren't completely knowledgeable on Singapore's intricacies, they are at least familiar with many of the country's pros and cons. For those from nations further afield, Singapore may be more of a surprise.

Either way, it's highly likely that you will experience some form of culture shock during your first months in Singapore.

Whilst this book doesn't aim to obliterate culture shock, it does provide you with information that will help you navigate your way to the other side of the culture shock ride. Having an early understanding of the Singapore culture will help you more easily make sense of, and enjoy, your new country.

# MAP OF SINGAPORE

The Republic of Singapore is made up one main island and 63 smaller islands and islets. Pulau Tekong, one of the largest of these smaller islands, which lies to the northeast of the main one, is not shown.

MALAYSIA

JOHOR STRAITS

SINGAPORE

SINGAPORE STRAIT

# CHAPTER 1

# FIRST IMPRESSIONS

> **❛**I don't know if you've ever noticed this, but first impressions are often entirely wrong.**❜**

**— Lemony Snicket,
'The Bad Beginning'**

If you ask a group of people what they know about Singapore, they will more than likely mention some of the following:

- It's squeaky clean
- It's full of high-rise buildings
- The transport system is excellent
- Drug dealers get the death penalty
- Hawker food is delicious and cheap
- People who are found guilty of graffiti are caned
- The weather is humid and hot
- Chewing gum is banned
- The shopping is excellent
- The airport is one of the best in the world
- Raffles Hotel

If the group contains expats you'll possibly hear that the country is considered to be 'Asia for beginners' or 'Asia light'.

Singapore undoubtedly creates an excellent first impression. Changi Airport is a true masterstroke of organisation and efficiency, which has resulted in many awards lauding it as 'World's Best Airport'. Immigration and luggage collection are more likely to be easier in Singapore than in most other airports around the world. Set one foot outside the airport doors and—BANG—Singapore's famed humidity will whack you in the chest. Sweating begins immediately.

In our first weeks living in Singapore my husband asked a colleague when he would acclimatise and stop sweating. "About five minutes after you're on the plane home" was the response. So, if you're moving to Singapore, or thinking of moving to Singapore, be warned that sweating is part of the deal! From my experience you never really acclimatise but you do learn to accept it as part and parcel of living in Singapore. You learn what sort of fabrics to wear, you carry an umbrella everywhere and try to avoid being outside during the hottest times of the day.

And take showers. Lots of showers.

During your first weeks in Singapore you'll get to see almost everything on that preconceptions list, although I sincerely hope you don't encounter corporal and capital punishment. If you opt for a taxi ride to where you're staying, you'll see that the preconception of being a country filled with high-rises is mostly true. What you can't see from the taxi are the other types of housing tucked away from the freeways. If you choose to catch the MRT to wherever you're staying on your first night then you'll get to experience a whole new level in public transport efficiency. A stroll to the hawker market will confirm that the food is both delicious and cheap. A trip along Orchard Road with all of its glitzy shopping malls and scarcely any litter will attest to the country's love of both shopping and cleanliness.

You won't see on first glance, and perhaps will never see, the workings of the Singapore criminal justice system but the feeling of safety and the absence of graffiti is testament to its effectiveness. As much as corporal and capital punishment seem distasteful to those of us who come from countries where these are outlawed, it results in a safe and respectful society that attracts many expats to live and work here.

The safety of Singapore and the criminal justice system are undeniably linked.

This safety and cleanliness does have a flipside and it's these elements which will often be the cause of the 'Asia for beginners' or 'sterile' labels from those that prefer a much grittier Asian experience. In 1993, writer William Gibson referred to Singapore as 'Disneyland with the death penalty'. Implicit in this backhanded compliment is that Singapore is Disney-perfect—a glossy veneer with no substance. Nothing could be further from the truth. Singapore is as complex as any other nation on earth; it just isn't as upfront about it. Gibson claims he went looking for the 'wrong side of the tracks' but that he couldn't find it as everything had been ripped down and rebuilt. I'd suggest Gibson didn't try hard enough. Perhaps if he'd move away from Orchard Road for a minute and volunteered for any number of organisations helping out with the problems found in any society (poverty, gambling, alcohol, domestic violence) he may have liked the place. If you limit yourself to what you see in the tourist brochures, then you may well find Singapore to be sterile. If you engage with the local population and move beyond the expat bubble, you'll find plenty to feed your need for a true Asian experience.

Singapore is all of those things in the list mentioned on the previous page.

For me, it wasn't the things on the list that created lasting first impressions. Rather it was the unexpected things that still stick in my mind from those early days almost five years later. Seeing workmen sitting unrestrained in the back of open trucks. The lack of power outlets in bathrooms (although the futility of blow-drying my hair in such a humid climate soon meant this lack was redundant!). The worship of electronic devices, particularly on public transport. The speed of the whole country and particularly of spoken language. Police are rarely seen, which surprised me as Singapore is known as a city of rules and penalties.

Whilst these are a few of my own first impressions I know that a first impression is usually not a true impression. It's part of the story but not the whole story. With Singapore if you scratch the Westernised surface you'll find a true Asian city with all the good and bad points that belong to any city in the world. The Asian heart of Singapore isn't immediately noticeable like it is in many other Asian cities. If you're from an English-speaking country the signs in English and dealing primarily with English-speaking people you may think that Singapore is not so different from home. This is good and bad. It's good as it can make for an easier transition initially and calm the nerves of the anxious expat. However, it can also lull the new arrival into thinking that everything in Singapore will work exactly the same way it does at home. When things don't work in line with how you think they should, then it can send you into a spin. 'But it looks a bit like home, so why doesn't it work the same way!' So, the lesson is to enjoy the first impressions you have of Singapore but always remember that Singapore is in Asia!

## CULTURE SHOCK

The term 'culture shock' is thrown around casually but it is a very real experience. Indeed, it almost brought me undone during our first fifteen months in Singapore, despite my enthusiasm and eagerness to move here. In much the same way that devouring every single book ever written about newborn babies can never fully prepare you for parenthood, no amount of reading and research will truly prepare you for

the transition from moving from your home country to your new one. You might talk the talk but you will trip over walking the walk. For some it will be a short trip but for others the trip lasts a while longer, and even then they may walk on shaky legs. As much as you may think you are prepared to embrace all of the new experiences of your new country, there will undoubtedly be days where 'novel and exciting' become 'too much and overwhelming'.

Culture shock is an emotional response to finding yourself in a new location with a new culture. You are disconnected from your surroundings. It doesn't necessarily have to involve moving to a new country. In hindsight, I can see that I suffered culture shock when I moved from a small, country town in one Australian state to a large capital city in another state. It's no coincidence that the year immediately following this move within Australia and also my first year living in Singapore, were two of the biggest tests in my relationship with my partner. Culture shock can be hard. The plus side of having culture shock in a country like Singapore is that with such a large expatriate population you are not alone. There is a lot of support available to help you through the process.

Culture shock is a well-documented process. There is a fairly predictable set of stages that people move through as they adjust to living in a new culture.

The first stage is the 'honeymoon stage', which is similar to being on holiday as everything is shiny, new and exciting. You are bubbling with enthusiasm. All of the differences with your home country are thrilling, but sadly that won't last forever.

The next stage is dramatically titled 'disintegration' or 'crisis' stage, and the differences that so charmed you a short while ago will now irritate you beyond belief. The chatty taxi uncles that you initially found hilarious and interesting will now make you grind your teeth and long for a moment of silence. The thought of having to make a phone call and deal with the inevitable language and accent difficulties will make you weep. This phase is more than just irritation and a yearning for your old life as culture shock has physical side effects that can affect your quality of life. Personally, I had trouble sleeping during this time and also became withdrawn,cocooning myself at home away from all that was 'new'. Other responses to this phase can range from weepiness, moodiness, resentment and anger. Some people begin to list a never-ending stream of all the things that are wrong with their new country whilst idealising their home country. It's important to note that everyone will react differently. Culture shock isn't the same for everyone.

It's entirely possible that the behaviour you adopt through the disintegration phase could become a habit, so it's best nipped in the bud. The best way to make this phase as short as possible is to force yourself out and about. Even the least social person needs to have a friend or two and hiding at home won't help you form new friendships. By seeking out friendships and connections with other people you will feel less alone and some of the initial enthusiasm of the honeymoon phase may reappear. I'm not advocating everybody to turn into social butterflies, but if you find activities that you enjoy, it is more than likely that you'll meet like-minded people (see Chapter 7 for some ideas).

Once you've pretty much mastered all of the basics of day-to-day life, you'll be in the autonomy stage. By now you can pretty much work everything out for yourself. You understand a lot of why your new country works the way it does, and if you don't understand the reasons you do accept them. Life in Singapore has a routine and things that once made you irrationally irritated are now just part of everyday life.

The final stage, independence, is one that not everyone will reach as it's typified by being integrated into the local community. In a place like Singapore that has such a large expat community, it is possible to live entirely separate to the local population. It's quite rare to find someone who fully meets this stage.

So, the good news is that you will adjust to your new culture. The bad news is that if or when you return 'home' you get to do the whole process again!

# CHAPTER 2

# GEOGRAPHY AND HISTORY

**❝Once**
**There was a beautiful island,**
**With a name.**
**You must believe me**
**When I say that sunlight,**
**Impure but beautiful,**
**Broke upon the bay, silvered**
**The unrepentant, burning moon.❞**

**— Edwin Thumboo**

## GEOGRAPHY AND CLIMATE

Singapore is typically divided into five regions:

- The **central** region incorporates the Central Business District (CBD) and the key tourist attractions but also stretches to the east coast, north to Macritchie Reservoir, and west up to Tiong Bahru. The CBD occupies the area to the south along the Singapore River, although businesses operate all over the island with many deliberately setting up offices further afield to save money on rent.

- The **east** region is dominated by Changi Airport as well as the northern part of the east coast including Tampines, Pasir Ris and Bedok.

- The **north** region takes in the central water catchment areas, the naval area around Sembawang, and Woodlands, which is where the causeway to Malaysia is situated.

- The **northeast** region lies between the east and north regions and includes ang Mo Kio, Serangoon, Punggol and the northeast islands such as Pulau Ubin.

- Lastly, the **west** region spreads from Clementi to Tuas, where the second causeway to Malaysia is located. It also includes the western water catchment area, the Jurong industrial areas and the western islands.

These facts are all well and good, but what do they mean? Firstly, being just one degree of latitude north of the equator means living in the tropics, and living in the tropics means that you should be prepared for rain, heat and humidity. All three simultaneously is common. It also means that Singapore doesn't experience the typhoons that much of tropical Southeast Asia faces on an annual basis.

While the thunderstorms may give you a fright, widespread damage is uncommon. Indeed, Singapore is quite fortuitously positioned so that it avoids much of the natural phenomena that wreaks havoc in Asia. It is not near any geological fault lines, so it isn't prone to earthquakes (although the occasional tremor from activity in Indonesia has been felt) and as the island is protected to the south by Sumatra it was spared the devastation caused by the 2004 tsunami throughout much of Southeast Asia.

Whilst Singapore may be a small country, it used to be even smaller! Its land mass has grown as a result of land reclamation projects. In 1960, the mainland was just

581 square kilometres, but today it is about 130 square kilometres larger. Land reclamation is also the reason why Singapore is so flat today as much of the landfill used for the reclamation projects came from the hills around the island. The bulk of the land has been developed in some manner, with only 5 per cent being forests or nature reserves.

Whilst this may seem a miniscule amount, Singapore has never had a huge abundance of natural resources to call upon and even in pre-colonial times the island was used for its location rather than for its resources. There is now very little delineation between urban and rural in Singapore, which is why the country is often referred to as a 'city-state'. However, it's not all wall-to-wall skyscrapers as there has been very careful town planning to ensure that there are ample green spaces across the island.

As far as I'm concerned, Singapore has two distinct seasons: 'blazing hot and very humid' from March until October-ish, or just hot and humid during the 'winter' period of October until February. However, meteorologists will argue that Singapore's weather is driven by two monsoon seasons: the Northeast Monsoon and the Southwest Monsoon.

The Northeast Monsoon season is from December until March, and has two separate weather patterns. The first is the wet phase of December and January which typically involves lots of rain in the

In 2014, the dry phase of the Northeast Monsoon season saw an extended period of dry weather with barely a drop of rain falling for an unprecedented eight weeks. Spaces that are usually lush and green turned brown and crackly. Tree ferns withered. Huge storm water drains dried up, as did the lake in the Botanic Gardens. It was as close to a drought as Singapore has ever experienced. Fortunately, for most years the dry phase of the Northeast Monsoon season is much shorter.

late afternoons and early evening. In my experience, this usually coincides with the arrival of the school bus sending kids home! The dry phase of February and March is the most comfortable weather you'll find in Singapore. The humidity drops (slightly), there's minimal rain and sometimes there's even a breeze!

The Southwest Monsoon season from June to September typically means showers and storms from the early hours of the morning until midday. Thunderstorms rarely last longer than thirty minutes, but there is the occasional day of intermittent showers. These storms are known as 'Sumatran squalls' as they form overnight in Sumatra before moving northward to Singapore. These are my least favourite storms as they often roll in around 4 am or 5 am and wake me up!

In between the two monsoon seasons are shoulder seasons, where you can expect pretty much any weather. Whilst this is the broad annual weather patterns for the area, Mother Nature often goes off-script so you should always carry an umbrella! Umbrellas are a multi-purpose item in Singapore. You can use it to hide from the sun and also protect yourself from the rain! Sometimes you can do both within the space of 15 minutes.

The upside of perpetual summer is that you never have to check the weather forecast before deciding what to wear each day!

Unfortunately, Singapore is at times shrouded in smoke haze that blows across the island from various different locations in Indonesia or Malaysia. It's usually the result of

either forest fires or burning in palm plantations, which is the preferred (i.e. cheap) land-clearing method of some plantation owners. In June 2013, the haze reached seriously unsafe levels for about a week. Official readings peaked in excess of 400 on the Pollution Standards Index (PSI), which meant the air quality was in the hazardous zone. People took to wearing face masks, such as the N95 mask, to avoid inhaling the smoke. Those who could leave the country did so until the situation eased. In 2015, Singapore experienced a very prolonged period of smoke haze, which lasted for several weeks. Although the readings were not as high as in 2013, they did pass into the hazardous level, which resulted in all national schools being closed for a day. During these times it's important to adhere to the advice of professionals and limit your time outside or wear the correct face mask if you can't avoid being outdoors.

## HISTORY

The common historical narrative of Singapore is that it was once a swamp and now it's a city-state of skyscrapers. This is somewhat true as Singapore has always been swampy, but that's true of any country in the topics. However, viewing pre-colonial Singapore as nothing more than a swamp simplifies the culture and history that has lived and thrived here for centuries before colonisation.

### Timeline

**1299**  Sri Tri Buana establishes the Kingdom of Temasek.

**1320**  Ships from the Chinese Yuan court visit Temasek to buy elephants. A Temasek delegation repaid the visit several years later.

**1330**  Wang Dayuan, a Chinese traveller, visits and notes that there are two separate settlements in Temasek. Pirates inhabit the area around Longyamen, whilst traders are seen on 'Banzu'—probably the hill now known as Fort Canning.

**1347** Sri Tri Buana dies; is succeeded by his son, Raja Kecil Besar. Siamese warships allegedly attack Temasek.

**1360** Invasion by Majapahit forces.

**1362** Raja Kecil Besar dies and is succeeded by Raja Muda.

**1374** Raja Muda dies. Damia Raja takes over.

**1390** Parameswara (AKA Iskandar Shah) invades Temasek, kills Damia Raja and takes control of Temasek.

**1398** Parameswara is driven from Temasek by either Majapahit or Siamese forces. He withdraws to Melaka where he establishes the Kingdom of Melaka in 1402.

**1611** Trading post at the mouth of the Singapore river burnt to the ground by Portuguese invaders.

**1703** The Sultan of Johor offers Singapura as a gift to a British sea captain, Alexander Hamilton. He declines.

**1819** Sir Thomas Stamford Raffles signs a treaty with the Sultan of Johor to establish a trading port along the Singapore River. Farquhar is appointed to run it.

**1822** Raffles returns. Dismisses Farquhar and implements the Jackson Plan.

**1824** The Sultan of Johor cedes the island of Singapore to Britain in perpetuity.

**1827** Establishment of the Straits Settlement.

**1867** Straits Settlement becomes a Crown Colony of Britain.

**1915** Feb 15: Singapore Mutiny.

**1942** Feb 15: Singapore falls to the Japanese.

**1945** August 14: Japan surrenders.

**1948** March 20: A limited election is held and won by the Singapore Progressive Party.

**1950** 18 people killed in the Maria Hertogh riot.

**1955** Partial self-rule granted. David Marshall becomes Chief Minister of Singapore.

Hock Lee bus riot; four people killed.

**1956** Chinese Middle school riots kill 13.

**1959** Full self-rule granted. General election is held and won by the People's Action Party (PAP).

Lee Kuan Yew becomes Prime Minister.

**1963** Singapore merges with peninsular Malaya, Sarawak and north Borneo to form the Federation of Malaya.

**1964** Two separate outbreaks of race riots; 36 deaths.

**1965** August 9: Singapore becomes the Republic of Singapore after being expelled from the Federation of Malaya.

September 21: granted membership in the UN.

December: Yusof bin Ishak becomes President.

**1967** Singapore becomes a founding member of ASEAN.

**1969** Race riots break out; four deaths.

**1971** Last British military forces leave Singapore.

Dr Benjamin Sheares becomes President.

**1981** C V Devan Nair becomes President.

**1984** Two opposition MP's win seats in Parliament.

**1985** Wee Kim Wee becomes President.

**1990** Goh Chok Tong becomes Prime Minister.

**1993** Ong Teng Cheong becomes the first popularly elected President.

**1999** S.R. Nathan succeeds Ong as President.

**2003** Free trade agreement signed with the US.

SARS outbreak occurs.

**2004** Lee Hsien Loong becomes Prime Minister.

Lee Kuan Yew becomes Minister Mentor.

**2011** Dr Tony Tan is elected President.

| 2013 | Little India riots occurs. |
| | Public protests over population expansion plans outlined in the government's 'White Paper'. |
| 2015 | Former Prime Minister Lee Kuan Yew dies, aged 91. |

## Longyamen, Temasek and Singapura

The island now known as Singapore has been called a variety of names, often in the same time period. The first written record of Singapore appears in 3rd century BC in a Chinese account that mentions *Pu Luo Chang*, which literally means 'island at the end'. Some of the earliest records mention the granite outcrop that once stood at the entrance to Keppel Harbour as Longyamen or 'Dragon's Tooth Gate', which

served as a navigational tool for early traders. In 1320, the Chinese Yuan court sent a mission to Longyamen requesting elephants, which were the Emperor's favourite animals. It's not known whether the request was fulfilled but it is known, thanks to the written records of the Yuan court, that a few years later a party from Longyamen visited China. The island was known as Temasek in written records dating from the mid-14th century, by which time the Javanese Majapahit empire was looking to conquer the island in order to control trade in the area. A poem written in 1365 by the Majapahit court confirms that the island then belonged to Java, but by 1400 the island had undergone another name change (Singapura) that may have been the result of either the Javanese or Siamese invaders.

## Lion City

The most famous of Singapore's folk tales centres on how Singapore became known as the 'Lion City'. The story goes that sometime in the 13th century, Sri Tri Buana, ruler of Palembang in Sumatra, set off to search for somewhere to establish a new city in the north-east. He spied a land with a beautiful white, sandy beach and was told by one of his advisers that it was called Temasek. Some versions of the story report that there then blew up a huge storm, with the seas becoming treacherous, preventing them from reaching land. Sri Tri Buana calmed the seas by throwing his crown into the water and they landed on Temasek, where a strange creature was spotted. It had a red body and a black head and moved quickly. The chief adviser informed his ruler that this was a lion, and Sri Tri Buana decreed that the land would be known as Singapura or the 'Lion City'.

## Sleepy Seaside Village?

Much of Singapore's early history has been lost to the ravages of time; however, what is known is that there were civilisation and trade by the 14th century. Since 1984, a series of archaeological digs at various sites have unearthed many artefacts dating from different times and countries that prove that Singapore has been an important international trading post for at least 700 years. The most well-known of these archaeological sites is in Fort Canning Park and the site now hosts a small museum about the project. At the beginning of 2015, a similar dig occurred at Empress Place, which uncovered more than 2,500 kg of artefacts dating from the 14th century and originating from as far away as India and China. The archaeological evidence reveals that the area around the Singapore River has been inhabited since at least the 14th century, and that some form of cultural exchanges occurred with China, Vietnam, India, and Thailand. Whilst it is early days in the assessment of the pieces found at Empress Place, the type of Chinese ceramics found were made from about 1375 to 1425, and were given by the Chinese Emperor to overseas leaders. These findings have lead archaeologists and historians to conclude that the island probably had an established government with a head of state during the late 14th and early 15th centuries.

Whilst there were few written accounts of Singapore after Iskandar Shah was chased from the island, the waters around the Straits of Melaka remained a thriving and fiercely contested waterway. Naval fleets from Portugal, Aceh, Holland, and Johor all used the area around Changi Point to ambush one another throughout the 15th and 16th centuries. The rulers may have moved away but the island was still inhabited and trade continued. Portuguese accounts from the 16th century record the names of villages such as Tanah Merah, Sungei Bedok, and Tanjung Rhu which are still used today, indicating the presence of Portuguese in the area. Ming Dynasty ceramics have also been found, which indicates trade with China continued through this 'silent' period and contradicts the common belief that Singapore was in decay throughout the 15th and 16th centuries. So important was Singapore as a port that in about 1611 the Portuguese razed the trading post at the mouth of the river to the ground.

## The Singapore Stone

Once upon a time, at the mouth of the Singapore River where the Fullerton Hotel now stands, stood a large rock that measured more than 2 metres wide and 1.5 metres high. The rock was inscribed in a strange language that has never been definitely identified, but may have been either an ancient Javanese or Sinhalese script. In 1843, the boulder was blown up and fragments were taken away to Calcutta. One of these returned to Singapore and now resides in the National Museum, but the script still remains a mystery.

## Colonial Days

The man credited with being the founder of colonial Singapore, Sir Thomas Stamford Raffles, actually spent very little time on the island. He was employed by the East India Company and went looking in the southern Straits of Malacca for a trading post, as control of Malacca had been taken by the Dutch. Initially he was looking in the Riau Islands but quickly realised that the Singapore River would be a better place. He landed in Singapore on January 28, 1819, signed a treaty with the Sultan of Johor on February 6 and left the very next day. Raffles sketched out a broad outline for the new settlement but entrusted the logistics of establishing the settlement to his long-term sidekick Major William Farquhar. Raffles made a brief return to Singapore in May 1819 to deliver building

The office towers at Raffles Place on the south bank of the SIngapore River serve as a modern backdrop for the polymarble statue of Sir Stamford Raffles, said to mark where he first landed in 1819.

materials but wouldn't return for another 3.5 years.

During Raffles' absence, trade flourished, aided by Raffles' instruction that Singapore should be a free trade port open to all. When Raffles returned in 1822, he found that Farquhar followed some of his blueprint but not all. He was dismayed to find that Farquhuar had raised revenue by instituting a licensing system for gambling as well as for the sale of alcohol and opium. Farquhar had also allowed the building of Chinese and Malay dwellings on the Padang and north bank of the river, which Raffles had designated as being reserved for European development. The third major point of contention was that Farquhar had permitted the slave trade to continue in the port, despite it being outlawed by the British Empire.

Despite being unwell and grief-stricken over the recent death of two of his three children, Raffles developed the

Jackson Plan. This plan was an urban redevelopment plan which set out separate areas for the various ethnicities living in Singapore, and is still the basic blueprint for the urban planning of the area surrounding the Singapore River. Raffles set about bringing the colony up to his ideals by abolishing the slave trade and raising taxes on alcohol, gambling and opium. Farquhar was replaced by Dr John Crawfurd, who signed a treaty shortly thereafter that extended British control to most of the island. In 1824, the Sultan ceded the island to the British East India Company in perpetuity.

In the following decades, Singapore established itself as a crucial trading port in the area. What made Singapore attractive was its free-trade status, which gave it great advantage over other ports in the area. The rise of the rubber and tin trades in Malaysia, the invention of steamships and the opening of the Suez Canal all combined to make Singapore a thriving trading port.

The population of the island grew alongside commerce, and by the end of the 19th century was already a multicultural society with Chinese, Malays, and Indians amongst the population. However, the island wasn't without problems. The population had quadrupled but the civil service hadn't grown in response and society was becoming increasingly lawless. Alcohol, opium, prostitution and gambling were rampant; with a scant police force, nothing much could be done to stop it. The establishment of the Straits Settlement in 1827 saw a stronger administrative presence in the region that brought some (but not all) of the unsavoury aspects of Singapore under control.

The colony continued to grow and prosper throughout the late 19th century and early part of the 20th century. World War I occurred, but it was confined to the other side of the globe and so it had very little impact upon Singapore. However, the war did prompt England to establish a naval base in Singapore as a defensive strategy should there be another war.

## The Japanese Occupation

On February 15, 1942, Singapore fell to the Japanese. The late Lee Kuan Yew describes this period of Singaporean history as "the dark ages… it was brutal (and) cruel". Despite having been considered an impenetrable fortress, Singapore was woefully under-resourced compared to the Japanese. Whilst a naval base had been established decades earlier, Britain had most of its forces fighting against Germany in Europe and the ships that it did have positioned off the Malayan coast were sunk by the Japanese in December 1941. Allied troops were chased down the Malay Peninsula by the Japanese. With nowhere else to retreat to, the Allies fought bitter battles in Singapore for over a week before surrendering. Until recently much of the physical history from these battles has lain undiscovered around Singapore, but battlefield archaeologist Jon Cooper has headed The Adam Park Project since 2009. The project aimed to uncover artefacts still lying around the Adam Park estate and use them to fill in some of the missing gaps in the history of these battles. These artefacts have been used to corroborate the written accounts of some aspects of both the fall of Singapore and life in captivity under the Japanese.

Life in Singapore changed dramatically under Japanese rule. In the first days of the occupation, the Japanese launched a reign of terror to display their might, which included a series of beheadings. The severed heads were displayed around the island as a warning of what would happen to those who did not obey their rules. Europeans were herded into camps, the country was renamed Syonan-to, new currency was issued, and rationing was introduced. As the years of occupation crawled by, the list of rationed items grew ever longer, leaving the local population to develop creative solutions in order to feed themselves. Rationing also created a thriving black market. The last two years of the occupation were particularly difficult, with the average death rate doubling, as a result of disease and malnutrition, compared to the decades before and after the war.

## Sook Ching Massacre

For several weeks from February 21,1942, Chinese males aged between 15 and 50 were ordered to attend mass screenings at various locations throughout the island. This became known as *sook ching* in Chinese, which means purification through elimination. The Japanese used these screenings to eliminate anyone they felt was a threat to Japan, or had been involved in anti-Japanese activities. China and Japan had a long history of discord and this is reflected in the specific targeting of the Chinese community. (Although it wasn't only the Chinese who experienced persecution by the Japanese, as almost a hundred Malay people who had worked with the British forces were executed at Pasir Panjang.) There were no clear guidelines for the screenings and those who passed the screening later said that luck played more of a part in this than any other factor. Those who didn't pass the screening were taken away and shot, with the bodies dumped either in the sea or in mass graves. Japanese records put the number of men killed during this time at 5,000 but the figure is believed to have been much higher than this.

The Former Ford Factory, where the Allied surrender was signed, is a museum that focuses upon life in Singapore during the years of the Japanese Occupation. It includes interviews, photographs, documents, as well as a recreation of the room in which the surrender was signed. It's well worth a visit to understand more about Singapore under Japanese rule.

## Toward Independence

The Japanese occupation of Singapore officially ended on September 4, 1945, although British forces did not land until the following day. The immediate period following the surrender was tumultuous. Looting and anti-Japanese sentiment were widespread. The two years before Singapore was declared a Crown Colony in 1947 were turbulent, with food shortages and a lack of infrastructure making life difficult.

Although modern Singapore has a reputation for having a peaceful and harmonious society, this hasn't always been the case. The 1950s and 1960s were a time of great tension and this spilt over into several riots during these decades. The mid-1950s saw a series of riots with a variety of root causes. The Maria Hertogh riot of December 1950 occurred after the courts awarded custody of a Dutch girl (Maria Hertogh), who had been raised by a Muslim foster mother, to her biological parents. The riots lasted for three days, with 18 people being killed and 173 injured, and the targets of the anger were mainly Europeans and Eurasians. A curfew was imposed for two weeks after the riot. On May 13, 1954, there was a riot that arose from a protest against compulsory National Service for male citizens. A year later, four people were killed in the Hock Lee bus riot of May 12, 1955. The riot's origins were an earlier strike by the workers of Hock Lee Bus Company. Tensions grew. On May 12, when the protesters refused to disperse, the police used high-pressure water-cannons on the mob. At the end of it, four people were dead and 14 were injured. In 1956, the Chinese Middle School riots took the lives of 13 people when widespread rioting erupted over the crackdown on pro-Communist organisations.

The civil unrest continued in the 1960s, with four people killed in a revolt on the penal island of Pulau Senang. In

1964, there were two separate outbreaks of race riots, each involving Malay and Chinese people. The first took place in July and resulted in the deaths of 23. Over 450 were injured. In September, tensions flared again after a Malay trishaw rider was killed in Geylang. The attacker was thought to have been of Chinese heritage. Thirteen people lost their lives in this riot.

The result of these tumultuous years has had a far-reaching affect upon Singapore. It highlighted the difference in approach between Malaysia and Singapore to race. Malaysia favoured Malays over other ethnicities, while Singapore felt a meritocracy approach was better, especially considering its population was almost 70 per cent Chinese. Eventually, the issue of race in combination with other factors lead Malaysia to expel Singapore from the Federation of Malaya in 1965.

Amidst all of this civil turmoil, Singapore continued on a path toward Independence. The first step came in 1955 when partial self-rule from Britain was granted. Full self-governance would not begin until 1959 and this transformed Singapore

from a Crown colony, where all legislation and administration was controlled by Britain, to creating its own Constitution and forming a government. The first full general election was held in 1959 and the People's Action Party (PAP) won 43 of the 51 seats and have remained in power ever since.

In 1961, Singapore joined the Federation of Malaya, which unified Singapore with peninsula Malaya, Sarawak, and North Borneo but this would be short-lived. There were deep ideological differences and a level of distrust between Singapore and Malaysia that could not be overcome, and Singapore left the union on August 9, 1965, to become an independent country.

## The Republic of Singapore

Much of the change that has occurred in the early years of independence was shaped by the threat of communism and the need to quell racial conflict. Pro-Communist forces from Indonesia had been behind some of the riots and the PAP set about enacting strict laws to sever their influence on the republic. Similarly, legislation was passed that specifically forbade racial and religious persecution. All of these elements combined to create a more harmonious society.

Since August 9, 1965, Singapore has moved forward at a rapid pace. The PAP's primary aims were—and still are—jobs, homes, health and education. Arguably, these are (or indeed should be!) the primary aims of all governments. However it hasn't all been plain sailing. The early days of independence were difficult, and further race riots took place in 1969. The government instigated a great deal of change and its list of accomplishments is lengthy. In economic terms, the Gross Domestic Product rose, unemployment fell, international trade grew, and tourism exploded. Singaporeans now have

longer life expectancy, increased literacy, superannuation plans, world-class health facilities, minimal environmental pollution, access to subsidised public housing and a transport system that is the envy of most other countries.

Some of the key areas of strength for Singapore are education, housing, and transport. The Singaporean education system is a world leader, particularly in maths and science. Global education surveys that rank nations on their education standards routinely rank Singapore's system in the top five or so countries around the world. Housing over five million people on a small island is no mean feat. Achieving this with a high standard of living is even harder. However, through careful planning and forethought, the Singapore government has ensured that every Singaporean has access to affordable, well-constructed housing. Whilst this scheme had its origins in the 1920s under British rule, it was after Independence that the scheme really took off. Today over 80 per cent of Singaporeans live in Housing Development Board (HDB) flats, with most owning them. The public transport system in Singapore is the envy of most other countries. Trains and buses are clean, regular and cheap. If you've come from a country whose public transport system is not

Creating affordable housing was one of the earliest aims of the government in the early years of Independence. Back then, many Singaporeans lived in sub-standard and unhygienic houses and the Housing Development Board (HDB) scheme began to build multi-storey public housing blocks to accommodate the growing population. Today over 80 per cent of Singaporeans live in HDB flats, with an impressive 90 per cent ownership.

particularly efficient or cheap, then you are in for a treat! The long-term aim is for every resident to be within a 10-minute walk of an MRT station.

It would be reasonable to note that most of these achievements have been made easier by the stability of the government. By having the same party in power for fifty years, Singapore has been able to follow through with plans, uninterrupted by a change in the ruling party. This stability of government makes Singapore an anomaly in Southeast Asia.

These achievements didn't come without sacrifices. The traditional way of living in *kampongs* disappeared, as did many traditional trades. Life went from being a fairly laid-back existence to being one of the most high-pressured lifestyles in the world. Personal freedom in Singapore is not on par with many other developed countries, but then Singapore is safer than most other countries as a result.

As Lee Kuan Yew stated "without the slightest remorse, that we wouldn't be here, we would not have made economic progress, if we had not intervened on very personal matters - who your neighbour is, how you live, the noise you make, how you spit, or what language you use. We decide what is right. Never mind what the people think." And as shown in the 2015 General Election, the majority of Singaporeans think that the positives in modern-day Singapore far outweigh the negatives!

## GOVERNMENT

After gaining independence in 1965, the Republic of Singapore adopted the Westminster model of government. The Head of State is the President and there are three branches of government: Executive, Legislative and Judicial.

- The Executive is the ministerial cabinet who are responsible for the day-to-day running of the country and government policy. It is comprised of ministers and led by the Prime Minister, who is appointed by the President.
- The Legislature is the parliament and is comprised of all ministers from the ruling party, who are elected by their constituents at general elections.
- The Judiciary is comprised of the Supreme and State Courts, and they administer the law independent to the Executive branch of government. The Chief Justice, Judges of Appeal, Judicial Commissioners and High Court Judges are appointed by the President, on recommendation by the Prime Minister. Jury trials were abolished in 1969, and judges preside on all cases.

Singapore's founding Prime Minister, Mr Lee Kuan Yew, died on 23 March 2015. So respected was Mr Lee that people were willing to queue for more than 11 hours to pay their final respects at Parliament House.

Presidential elections are held every six years, under the 'first past the post' system, where the winner is the candidate who receives the majority of the votes. General parliamentary elections are held every five years, but they can be held sooner if the President considers it advisable in consultation with the Prime Minister to dissolve the parliament earlier. Singapore has short and sharp election campaigns, with a minimum campaign period of just nine days between the announcement of the election and polling day. Voting is compulsory for all Singaporean citizens (this excludes Permanent Residents) over the age of 21.

Since 1959, when Singapore was granted self-rule, the People's Action Party (PAP) has held the balance of power. In the 2015 election, the PAP won 83 of the 89 parliamentary seats, an increase of two seats from the previous election. The government also granted the opposition three Non-Constituency Member of Parliament (NCMP) seats, which are given to members of opposition parties who are typically the best runners-up in the election. They provide alternative and independent viewpoints to parliamentary debates.

Singapore's Prime Minister is the highest-paid politician in the world, despite accepting a $700,000 pay cut in 2011. The Prime Minister currently earns an impressive $2.2 million per annum, while new ministers earn just over $1 million. Whilst this may seem excessive, political office comes with very few of the perks that are available for politicians in other nations, such as housing and private jets. As the old saying goes, 'if you pay peanuts, you'll get monkeys'—by pegging politician's salaries to those of the private industry it's hoped that the best people will enter politics. It is also thought that a large salary will make politicians less susceptible to the lure of corruption.

# CHAPTER 3

# THE PEOPLE OF SINGAPORE

> ❝You know the Singaporean. He is a hard-working, industrious, rugged individual. Or we would not have made the grade. But let us also recognise that he is a champion grumbler.❞
>
> **— Lee Kuan Yew**

Singapore is just about as multi-cultural as a country can be. Singapore is a true country of immigrants: apart from the Malay portion of the population, who were the original inhabitants, every single person's family tree began in another country. Not only is it a multi-cultural country but it is also multi-faith and multi-lingual, and Singaporeans take enormous pride in their social tolerance. With four official languages and multiple different religions, the people of Singapore set an example of peaceful co-existence for the rest of the world.

In 2014, Singapore was home to 5,469,700 people, with 3,343,000 of those being Singapore citizens. An additional 527,000 are Permanent Residents, which means that the balance of 1.6 million people are in the country working temporarily.

Singaporeans are generally broken into three racial groups: Chinese, Malay and Indian. In addition to these three groups, there are a couple of others that have distinct cultural differences to the main ethnic group to which they belong, namely the Peranakan and Eurasian communities. The largest section of Singapore's population is of Chinese heritage, with the Chinese community comprising 74.3 per cent of Singapore's citizens. A further 13 per cent of Singapore have a Malay background and the Indian popula over 9 per cent. The remaining 3.3 per cent come from a multitude of different backgrounds. Even after four years it still takes me aback to be asked for my race on forms, and while my Western instinct is to write 'none of your business' I dutifully tick 'other'. Labelling people is simply part of Singaporean culture with no malice intended. I like to think it's a way of acknowledging people's heritage and maintaining links to their traditional cultures.

Singapore wears its racial diversity and harmony as a badge of honour. In a region that is often fraught with racial, ethnic and religious tensions, Singapore is an example of tolerance. This does not mean that racial tensions don't exist. They most definitely do. However, the various pieces of legislation and Singaporean's innate characteristic of following rules mean that racism is not as overt as it may be in other places. Over my years here I can only think of two times that I have heard locals make derogatory remarks based on race or ethnicity, which is significantly less than what I would have encountered in my home country. They were muttered under the speaker's breath, and although neither remark was directed toward me, it gave me a glimpse into some of the underlying ethnic tensions that I would otherwise be oblivious to.

## THE SINGAPORE CHARACTER

As with any nationality, describing the key features of the Singaporean character is not easy but there are a couple of popular tongue-in-cheek stereotypes. The first is that every Singaporean aspires for 'The Five C's': cash, car, credit card, condo and country club. This stereotype taps into the idea that Singaporeans are driven by status and wealth, or that they are 'money face'. Certainly to afford all the 5 C's

a person would need to be very affluent – the car alone will cost more than $100,000! A taxi driver once told me that there are three cultures in Singapore: a complaining culture; a queueing culture; and a *kiasu* culture.

I can honestly say that I haven't picked up on the complaining part of Singapore's culture, but I think every nationality likes to have a good grumble every now and then. In the quote at the start of this chapter, even Lee Kuan Yew acknowledges that Singaporeans are 'champion grumbler(s)'. The queueing culture I have seen many times. Walking along New Bridge Road just before Chinese New Year (CNY) I saw a massive queue of people and assumed the MRT must've been out of action and this was the replacement bus queue. I was very wrong. It was, in fact, a queue for a *bak kwa* shop and the man at the head of the line told me he had been in line for five hours to buy his traditional CNY *bak kwa*. There was another *bak kwa* shop two doors away which had no queue but the man told me the queueing at this particular shop was a CNY tradition. If you happen to be near a McDonald's outlet on the day they release any sort of limited edition toy, then you will see this queueing culture in action! However, Singaporeans are very polite and respectful queuers. Everybody seems happy to await their turn and no-one tries to jump the queue (as far as I have seen).

The *kiasu* culture goes hand-in-hand with the queueing culture. *Kiasu* is a Singlish word that means something along the lines of 'fear of losing' and is a little like FOMO (fear of missing out). *Kiasu* is also the term that describes Singaporean's competitivenes. It can certainly be applied to life's big achievements but it's usually used to negatively

IF YOU'RE LAZY THE PRIME MINISTER WILL COME AND GET YOU.

describe the smaller, inconsequential 'wins'. Drivers who absolutely will not ever let you merge into their lane and will speed up to prevent this happening are *kiasu*. The person who has to be first through the doors on the MRT is displaying *kiasu* behaviour. Whilst it certainly has negative connotations, Singaporeans seem to wear it as a badge of honour, much the same as my own countrymen (Australians) are proud of their drinking ability. Many Singaporeans believe that only by having *kiasu* leaders has the country been able to achieve such monumental change in such a short time frame. So being *kiasu* is not always a bad thing!

Leaving aside the well-known stereotypes, there are a few other national characteristics of Singaporeans. They are fiercely and proudly patriotic. Patriotism is at its peak during July and August in the lead-up to National Day. Singapore flags are displayed by businesses, private flats and in public areas. But Singaporeans are also law-abiding citizens that dutifully take down their National Day decorations by September 30 each year in line with the law.

## National Service

National Service (NS) is compulsory for all male Singapore citizens, and also for second-generation Permanent Residents. Full-time NS lasts for two years, but this is shortened by two months for those who reach certain fitness standards. Basic training lasts for between three to six months. Most NS men will then serve in the Singapore Armed Forces (SAF), but there are also opportunities in the Police Force and the Civil Defence Unit. After completing full-time NS men are 'operationally ready' and they become part of Singapore's reserve forces until they are aged 50 for officers and aged 40 for other servicemen. This means they can be called up at any time to serve to a maximum of 40 days per year. Call-outs go out several times a year via the media, so if you see/hear random phrases such as 'Grey sharks', 'Leaping squirrels' on your TV screen or radio, don't panic! It's just the reservist code words. Conscientious objecting is not an option and failure to enrol for NS is punishable with fines, imprisonment, and/or the cancellation of citizenship or Permanent Residency status.

A Singaporean friend says that he believes Singaporeans can be reserved people until you get to know them, and I agree. I've rarely heard a loud Singaporean and I've always found Singaporeans to be respectful and polite.

Great emphasis is placed upon getting a good education in Singapore. Before moving here I had never heard of 'enrichment centres' but there is a whole industry set up to help students achieve the best exam results they can. I've never been able to figure out if the desire to do well at school is driven by wanting kids to achieve their fullest potential (*kiasu*?) or the fear of losing face. It's probably a combination of both. Either way, Singapore is a very result-driven culture.

I spoke to many Singaporeans to get an understanding of what they think are the common characteristics among their fellow citizens and the only common answer was social tolerance. Singapore is an amazingly tolerant society. No-one seems to be bothered by what race another person is, or what language they speak, or which faith they adhere to. These questions might be asked but no judgements will be made publically. It's true that the government have introduced laws to encourage social tolerance but I think there's an awareness amongst Singaporeans that other countries in their region have been torn about by intolerance and have come to the conclusion that despite being a 'multi' society the country is a much nicer to live in if everyone just gets along!

## SINGAPORE RESIDENTS

The bulk of the population of Singapore come from either Chinese, Malay or Indian heritage. It's important to acknowledge that the community as a whole is diverse but so, too, are each of the racial groups. Not all Chinese are

Buddhist, not all Indians are Hindu, and not all Malays are Muslim. Lots of Singaporeans from all ethnicities have no religious affiliation at all.

## The Chinese Population

The majority of Singaporeans, 74.3 per cent as of 2014, have Chinese ancestry. Chinese links to Singapore stretch back centuries, as the Ming Dynasty ceramics uncovered at the Empress Place archaeological dig in 2015 prove. Trade between China and Southeast Asia has a long history and it is probable that some traders chose to settle on the island before it was colonised by the British in the 19th century. During the colonial period, many Chinese traders came to Singapore to set up businesses as Singapore was considered a profitable place for traders due to its free trade policy. Early Chinese immigrants also included coolies who were involved in clearing the jungle and building the colony's early infrastructure. Life in colonial times wasn't as easy or as prosperous as many envisioned, with many returning to their homeland, but many stayed and prospered. Since colonial times, Chinese immigration to Singapore has been continual. Some Chinese Singaporeans have been here for many generations, while others only a generation or two.

Chinese Singaporeans predominantly come from five different ethnic groups: Hokkien, Teochew, Canton, Hakka,

I found out the hard way that not all Chinese Singaporeans speak Chinese when I encouraged my daughter to say *xie xie* (thank you) to an aunty. The aunty replied, "She speaks more Chinese than me!" I mention this because as a person living in another country it's very easy to fall into the trap of seeing your new country and its citizens as homogenous. Singapore has the same diversity as most major cities and you should always respect this.

and Hainan. Each of these regions has different languages or dialects, beliefs and traditions whilst also sharing many things in common. In the colonial area, each of the different ethnic groups were allotted different parts of Chinatown in which to live, and were often associated with particular occupations.

Chinese people traditionally have three characters to their names. The family name (or character) is written first, followed by the given name, usually in two parts. For example, current Prime Minister Lee Hsien Loong's given name is Hsien Loong, and Lee is his family name. These days many Chinese Singaporeans also have Westernised names in addition to their Chinese name.

Chinese Singaporeans belong to a variety of religions, with 57 per cent with the Buddhist faith and 14 per cent to Taoist in the 2010 census. Christianity was the third most popular religion, but just over one fifth reported that they belonged to no religion. Many of the Chinese traditions come from Chinese folklore or astrology and aren't part of any religious tradition. Chinese New Year, Hungry Ghost Festival,

### Ancestor Worship

Ancestor worship plays a prominent role in many Chinese family traditions and is linked to both Taoism and Buddhism. It is a way of showing filial piety (respect and honour) to one's ancestors. In times past when families lived in larger houses, each family would have an ancestral altar in their living hall, which housed an ancestral tablet with the names of deceased ancestors written on it. Some families also housed the urns holding their ancestors' remains in the ancestral altar. Joss sticks would be burnt on the altar and food offerings were also placed there. These days most people live in smaller places so an ancestral altar isn't practical. Some families still opt to have a very small altar, sometimes a small shelf with a photo of a revered ancestor. Today most Chinese people opt for cremation and the urn is either stored in a niche at a columbarium or at a temple. The offerings will then be carried out at either these locations or at the cemetery. Chinese have four main times when they observe ancestor worship: Chinese New Year, Qing Ming, Hungry Ghost, and the anniversary of the ancestor's death.

Qing Ming and the Mid-Autumn festivals all originated centuries ago in China and are linked to Chinese mythology

## The Malay Population

As Singapore is at the tip of the Malay Archipelago it's no surprise that the Malay people are the original inhabitants of Singapore. The term 'Malay' does not necessarily mean that all people who identify as Malay have heritage directly descended from what is now called Malaysia. Rather, Malay people come from various parts of the region surrounding Singapore including the Riau Islands, Java, Sulawesi and Sumatra. In 1824, people with Malay ancestry formed the largest part of the population, but today, they account for 13.3 per cent of the population.

Malay names traditionally have three parts: a given name, followed by either 'bin' (meaning 'son of') or 'binte' (meaning 'daughter of'), followed by the father's given name. For example, Yunos bin Iskander refers to 'Yunos, son of Iskander'. If Yunos has a son and names him Ahmad, the son's full name will be Ahmad bin Yunos. Generally, Malay people do not have family names but instead they attach their father's name to their given names.

The Malay portion of Singapore's population identify almost entirely as Muslim, with just over 1 per cent nominating another religion or no religion in the 2010 Census. The most common form of Islam in Singapore is Sunni.

## The Indian Population

The Indian population is, at 9.1 per cent, the smallest ethnicity in Singapore, but there has been a small but noticeable increase in recent years. Whilst 'Indian' is the word used to describe this ethnicity, not all Singaporeans actually have

Indian heritage. Rather, 'Indian' is used to describe those from the entire Indian subcontinent. This includes Sri Lanka (formerly Ceylon), Bangladesh and Pakistan. The vast majority (roughly 60 per cent) of modern Indian Singaporeans have a Tamil heritage from South India, which is why Tamil is one of Singapore's national languages. However, not all Indian Singaporeans speak Tamil as many speak Hindi and other regional dialects.

The first recorded arrival of Indian people to Singapore were the 'Lashkars', an army unit of soldiers from the Bengal army, who arrived with Sir Stamford Raffles in 1819. However, maritime trade had been occurring between the two regions for centuries so Indian people may have settled in Singapore before the arrival of Raffles. During the colonial era, the numbers of Indian people in Singapore increased dramatically. Between 1825 and 1872, the British transported Indian convicts to the island to clear the jungles and also to labour on building sites. The Istana and St Andrew's Cathedral, as well as most of the colonial roads were built using Indian convict labour. People from the Indian subcontinent were not employed just as convict labour as many moved to Singapore to work in all manner of roles during the colonial period, including the civil service. A traditional role of Indians in Singapore has been as moneychangers and this is still common today.

Name-giving in Indian culture has many variations, depending upon religion, caste and tradition. The format of names for Hindus varies depending upon where in India the family originates from. Many North Indians have the first name/middle name/surname format that's common in Western countries. Those who are Sikhs will have Singh as a surname if they are male, or Kaur if they are female. Tamil

Hindu's traditionally have no surname. Some Tamils will have their given name followed by their father's given name, with either s/o for 'son of' or d/o for 'daughter of' in between. However, this format is rare now. Other Tamil people will have the first initial of their father's name, followed by their given name. For example, S. Laxman, with the 'S' being the first letter of his father's name. The practice of only using the first initial was started to shorten what are sometimes quite long names.

Although Hinduism remains the most popular religion amongst Indian Singaporeans, they are affiliated with a variety of religions. After Hinduism the next most practiced faiths are Islam and Christianity, with smaller percentages observing the Sikhs and Janist faiths.

For four years it has puzzled me why I get called "Ms Kelly", rather than Ms Jackson-Nash, until I started writing this book. The answer is because Singapore has so many varied ways of writing names it's easier to just use the person's title followed by the first part of their name. With traditional Chinese and Malay names this is the correct way to address people.

## The Peranakans

The Peranakan people are also called the 'Straits Chinese', as the culture originated around Malacca with Chinese-born traders marrying local women. Over the centuries, the Peranakans have developed distinct cultural practices that are a unique blend of Chinese, Malay and English. Many of the Peranakans who settled in Singapore in the early years of the colony spoke English and this allowed them to establish profitable businesses and many of the elite in colonial Singapore were Peranakans.

Even today, Peranakan people have a distinct speaking pattern that blends English and Hokkein with Malay and has loose grammar rules. Whilst the number of Peranakan people who adhere strictly to the old traditions has dwindled, the Peranakan influence is evident throughout Singapore. Nonya food is the cuisine developed by the Peranakan 'Nonya's' (women) that is a blend of Malay and Chinese, but also draws influences from elsewhere in Asia and Europe. Peranakans are famous for their beautiful ceramics, silverware and embroidery. I long for a pair of embroidered Peranakan slippers! There are several areas of Singapore, like Katong, Joo Chiat and Emerald Hill that have houses built by Peranakans typified by their ornate, tiled exteriors. Baba House, on Neil Road, is a restored Peranakan home where there are regular tours conducted by the National University of Singapore. The Peranakan Museum in Armenian Street is well worth a visit to learn more about Peranakan culture.

### The Eurasians

Eurasian people are descendants of what used to be called 'mixed marriages', meaning marriages between an Asian and a European. Eurasians have a long heritage dating back to the 15th century when explorers and traders from Europe first came to Asia. Many of these men married Asian women and over time a distinct Eurasian culture developed, including new languages.

The languages have all but disappeared now, but the Eurasian traditions and values are still maintained. The influence of the European ancestor (who was often, but not always, male) meant that most of the Eurasian community follow Christianity and its associated birth, marriage and death rituals. The former President of Singapore,

Dr Benjamin H. Sheares was of Eurasian heritage, as are radio personalities Vernetta Lopez and Jean Danker.

The Eurasian Heritage Centre is on Ceylon Road and features a number of displays about different aspects of Eurasian culture.

## Permanent Residents

There are over 500,000 people living in Singapore who have been granted Permanent Resident (PR) status. Many expats who move to Singapore and decide to stay long-term apply for permanent residency for a variety of reasons that include increased stability, priority in the public school system, and greater tax incentives. In recent years, the number of PR passes granted has been decreasing as the Immigration and Checkpoints Authority (ICA) has tightened the requirements, but should you consider applying for PR status, you can find the details on the ICA website. National service is compulsory for the sons of PRs, and as such from the age of 13 they are required to get an Exit Permit from the government if they are leaving the country for longer than three months at a time. PRs are not required to vote in Singaporean elections.

## SINGAPORE NON-RESIDENTS

Over 1.6 million people living in Singapore are considered to be non-residents, meaning they are neither a Singapore citizen nor a permanent resident. This group represents all of the people who move to Singapore for work and fall in to two main categories: expatriates and migrant workers. To me, the difference between an expat and a migrant worker is that an expat, unlike a migrant worker, does not take up work in another country solely due to economic necessity.

Whilst an expat may choose to work away from their home country to earn a higher salary, this usually is not their only option for employment. Migrant workers, on the other hand, move to Singapore so that they can support their family in their home country.

A further difference is that expats, who are usually granted an EP, S Pass, or PEP (see overleaf), are permitted to bring their dependant family members with them to Singapore, whilst migrant workers cannot.

## Migrant Workers

Migrant (or transient) workers are those employed in low-to-medium skilled roles across a variety of industries such as construction, domestic work, manufacturing and the service industry. In 2012, migrant workers made up about 75 per cent of all foreigners working in Singapore. A sizeable but often overlooked section of the Singapore population, migrant workers are granted a Work Permit to work in Singapore and they contribute enormously by doing the manual jobs that keep the country running.

Male workers are usually from the Indian subcontinent, while female workers come from other Southeast Asian countries as well. Male migrant workers usually live in large dormitories that are dotted around the country and it's common to see many men all sitting in the back of open trucks being transported to and from their workplaces. Foreign Domestic Workers (FDW) are all female and they usually live in the household for which they work.

Although the migrant worker community in Singapore tends to stick to themselves, they have brought bits of their home cultures with them that add another dimension to Singaporean society.

It's important to be aware that migrant workers are not always treated fairly. Both domestic workers and labourers are occasionally taken advantage of and are often powerless to seek help or advice. Fortunately there are organisations such as Transient Workers Count Too (twc2.org.sg) and HOME (www.home.org.sg) that aim to help transient workers gain new skills and advice should the need arise.

## Expats

The term 'expatriate' is typically used to refer to professional or semi-professional workers who move from their home country to work in another country. Expats are usually employed on an Employment Pass (EP), Personalised Employment Pass (PEP), or S Pass. You may find more details on these different types of work pass on the Ministry of Manpower website (www.mom.gov.sg).

There are many different terms used to describe expats. Expats are known as 'foreign talent (FT)' but are also referred to as 'foreigners'. Sometimes, Singaporeans call Western expats *ang moh*, which comes from Hokkien and literally means 'red hair'. Originally, being called an *ang moh* by a Singaporean was not a compliment, although much is dependent upon the tone in which it was said. Over the years, *ang moh* has just become what Singaporeans sometimes call Westerners and it's usually not meant maliciously.

However, as mentioned before there are racial tensions in Singapore and some of this is aimed toward expats. As you will likely find in any country, there are some Singaporeans who believe that expats take the high-paying jobs that could be done by Singaporeans. The accuracy of this isn't for me to debate but it is something to be aware of during your time in Singapore. Thankfully much of this discontent is often confined, it seems, to the comments section of online news sites, so be prepared should you decide to read them!

## RELIGION

Singapore is a multi-faith society with most of the world's major religions being observed. Buddhism, Islam, Hinduism, Taoism, and Christianity are the predominant religions but there are also many other faith systems throughout the country. The Maintenance of Religious Harmony Act aims to maintain religious harmony throughout the country by preventing derogatory remarks and/or discussion about different religions, and by also having a clear separation of church and state. Both the Unification Church and the Jehovah's Witness are not permitted to operate in Singapore. The Unification Church is considered a cult, whilst the Jehovah's Witnesses were banned as they object to their followers participating in National Service. In the 2014 Census, almost 18 per cent of the population state that they follow no religion, and this percentage has been increasing with each census period. This tends to indicate that, as with many other countries, secularism is on the rise.

Singaporeans may observe more than one religion, as traditions and beliefs from other religions are often included alongside a main religion. In particular, many Chinese Singaporeans, while officially Buddhist, incorporate many of the teachings of Confucius into their belief system.

### Buddhism

Buddhism is the most popular religion in Singapore, with followers from all ethnicities. Buddhism began in India, but has been practiced in Southeast Asia since the 2nd century. Mahayana is the Buddhism variation usually followed in

Singapore. The type of Buddhism in Singapore is heavily influenced by the Chinese Buddhist philosophy which varies from the Indian form. Unlike Islam and Christianity which worship a god, Buddhism focuses upon a set of ethics called the 'Four Noble Truths', which were outlined in Buddha's first sermon. The four truths are:

- Dukkha: the truth of suffering;
- Samuda-ya: the truth of the origin of suffering;
- Nirodha: the truth of the cessation of suffering;
- Magga: the truth of the path to the cessation of suffering.

## Taoism

Like Buddhism, Taoism was brought to Singapore by early Chinese settlers. Founded by Laozi, the central Taoist belief is that people should have a calm mind and live in harmony with nature in order to live a good life. Buddhism and Taoism are often jointly practised, as many of the central beliefs align.

## Christianity

According to the 2010 Census, 18 per cent of Singaporeans belong to a Christian faith, spread over a number of different denominations. Christianity came to Singapore during the colonial times, with the British introducing the Church of England, whilst the Portugese introduced Catholicism. Christianity is based upon the Bible, and the beliefs that Jesus Christ is the son of God and that believers will ascend to Heaven after death. There are many Christian churches throughout Singapore, with many built during the Colonial era such as the Armenian Church, St. Andrew's Cathedral and the Cathedral of the Good Shepherd. Catholicism is the most popular form of Christianity throughout Singapore.

Kampong Glam is the Malay enclave of Singapore and the Masjid Sultan (or Sultan Mosque) stands proudly at its centre. The original mosque was built by Sultan Hussein from 1824–1826, but was completely rebuilt in 1924 to celebrate the centenary of the original mosque. The mosque was gazetted as a national monument in 1975.

## Islam

Arabic and Indian traders introduced Islam to Southeast Asia. Within the Malay population, almost 99 per cent of people follow Islam. The core ideas of Islam are recorded in the Qur'an, the central scared text. There are five pillars of Islam:

- Shahadah: declaring that there is no god but God, and that Allah is his messenger;
- Salat: praying five times per day;
- Zakat: donating a percentage of earning to the poor;
- Sawm: fasting during the month of Ramadan; and
- Hajj: making a pilgrimage to the Hajj once during a lifetime, finances permitting.

The end of Ramadan is celebrated with close relatives and friends on Hari Raya Puasa. In Singapore, some Muslim women choose to wear a headscarf and dress modestly as an outward symbol of their faith, while others don't. The oldest mosque in Singapore is Masjid Omar Kampong Melaka on Keng Cheow Street and dates from 1820. Islamic people eat a *halal* diet as prescribed by Islamic law. This includes the avoidance of pork products and alcohol as well using food prepared according to specific *halal* practices. In Singapore, suppliers and food outlets which are *halal* display *halal* certification certificates prominently.

## Hinduism

Hinduism spread from India to Singapore with the early Indian settlers. Unlike most other religions, people must be born into the Hindu faith as conversion is not possible. Hindusim is often cited as the world's oldest religion, and it is different to most religions as it does not have either a founder or a single text that outlines the religion's fundamental beliefs.

Rather, much of Hindu law has been recorded in various texts over time including the Vedas and the Upanishads. The Hindu faith teaches that the supreme God takes a variety of forms, which is why there are a variety of different gods worshipped in Hinduism. Hindus believe that every living thing has a soul and that they will be reborn after death, so many Hindus choose to eat a vegetarian diet. Most Hindus will visit the temple weekly and there are roughly thirty Hindu temples spread throughout the island. The Sri Mariamman Temple in Chinatown is the oldest Hindu temple, with the original wooden temple being built in 1827. Singapore's Hindu population observe many traditions throughout the year, with Deepavali being the largest celebration. Some Singaporean Hindu festivals, such as Thaipusam, are still celebrated in Singapore despite being out of fashion in India.

## LGBT Singapore

Despite male-to-male sexual intercourse being illegal under Section 377A of the Penal Code, Singapore has become much more accepting of alternative sexualities in the last decade. Whilst it may lag behind other countries with allowing same-sex marriage, there is a thriving LGBT community. The Internet has contributed greatly to this as it provides a safe space for people to express and explore their sexualities. There are several clubs throughout the island that host gay and/or lesbian parties on a regular basis, and the annual Pink Dot event is held to promote acceptance of LGBT people. A Singaporean friend says that in recent years public displays of affection (such as holding hands) have become acceptable, which indicates there is an increasing tolerance and acceptance of LGBT couples. Whilst couples may receive looks from passers-by, verbal or physical violence is almost unheard of, which is a testament to the tolerant and accepting nature of Singaporean society.

# CHAPTER 4

# SETTLING IN

> *If you reject the food, ignore the customs,*
> *fear the religion and avoid the people,*
> *you might better stay at home.*

**— James Michener**

For the expat living in Singapore, there are two distinct types of 'fitting in'. There is fitting in to the expat lifestyle and there is fitting in to the wider Singaporean society. It's entirely possible to live your whole time in Singapore within what is sometimes called 'the expat bubble': mixing only with other expats and interacting with Singaporeans only when necessary. Sticking with your own is a very normal human reaction to living outside of your home culture, and how much you choose to engage with the local people and culture is entirely up to you. However, meeting and getting to know the locals will add a richness to your time in Singapore as well as giving you a much truer picture of the country.

## SINGAPOREAN VALUES

When a country looks as much like a Western country as Singapore does, it's very tempting to assume that the value system will also be the same. However, the key to understanding much of how Singapore works is to be respectful of the very different underpinning values of society. As Singapore's respected first Prime Minister Lee Kuan Yew noted, "what Asians value may not necessarily be what Americans or Europeans value." The lack of appreciation for these different values has brought more than one expat undone.

## Harmony

The importance of group harmony over the rights of the individual is, perhaps, the most difficult Singaporean value to grasp for those who have lived in Western countries. In the West, the rights of the individual are far more important than those of the community as a whole. But in many Asian cultures, including Singapore, the good of the community is put before the needs of the individual.

This is not to say that individuals have no rights in Singapore, but just that if the communal good clashes with an individual's actions, the communal good will usually win. In effect, it's better to have a single upset person rather than the other way around!

As Singapore is a very small island that is home to a multitude of people from different cultures, religions, and languages, the government has had to be proactive to ensure that the country remains relatively harmonious. The laws developed to ensure societal harmony were accepted by the majority as Singaporeans could see that they benefited the common good, despite the fact that they undoubtedly limit some personal freedoms.

There are several pieces of legislation, which combined, mean that it is illegal to incite hatred toward others based upon their race or religion. These laws are not taken lightly and during my four years in Singapore I can think of at least three separate incidents where these laws were cited. The immediacy of social media has seen at least two foreign-born permanent residents of Singapore fall afoul of the Sedition Act by posting comments deemed to be racist on various social media platforms. The lesson here is to think twice before posting comments on social media!

## Family

The family is the backbone of Singaporean culture. For the Chinese, this stems from the long tradition of filial piety as outlined by Confucius, but it's also a theme that's deeply ingrained in both the Malay and Indian cultures as well. Whilst family is undeniably important to every culture, most Asian people feel a very deep obligation to the family unit, particularly to their elders. In broad terms, Asian people afford a greater respect and deference for their elders than is usual for many other cultures. Filial piety encourages respect for one's parents and older relatives, to take care of one's parents, to avoid doing anything that will bring shame upon the family name, and to honour deceased ancestors. So important is filial piety in Singapore that The Maintenance of Parents Act was introduced in 1995. It allows parents above the age of 60 who are unable to financially support themselves to seek maintenance through the courts from their children.

Multi-generational housing has been a long-standing lifestyle throughout Asia and is still common in modern Singapore. Some of the newer Housing Board (HDB) developments have specially designed flats that are effectively two flats in one. The family with kids can live in the large part, whilst the grandparents have a smaller flat next door with a connecting doorway. Very affluent families that can afford landed properties will often have room for more than one generation. Young Singaporeans tend to live with their parents for longer periods of time compared with other nationalities. This is partly because of duty to family and also because of the practicalities: Singapore property is very expensive and single people are unable to buy a HDB flat until they are 35. So, staying at home until you either marry or turn 35 and can buy your own flat seems to be the popular alternative to renting.

## 'Face'

'Face' is a word for respect and dignity that extends beyond the individual into the family. It's not an easy concept to describe but it's essentially the measure of a person's worth. You'll most likely hear it in the expression 'lose face'. To 'lose face' is to lose respect and is something that most Singaporeans will try and avoid at all costs.

When we first moved to Singapore, we had a very protracted house-leasing saga and when I expressed to my husband my extreme frustration that our property agent hadn't responded to my emotional emails, he replied that I shouldn't expect to hear from her until she had good news. To do otherwise would be seen as losing face, even though the situation was not of her making. This was an important lesson to learn early in my Singapore days. I quickly learnt that when I rephrased my emails to ask how the landlord had responded, as opposed to what the property agent had done, an answer would be given quickly as I wasn't putting her in a position where she would lose face.

## Hierarchy

Singapore is a meritocracy, where people advance through merit, but it also has very strong hierarchical relationships. People who are more senior, either by age or position, are accorded great respect. When making introductions, the eldest people in a group are usually introduced first. The same goes when serving food or drinks—the older people should be served first and have first choice of what's on offer. It's this respect for age and wisdom that is the reason many people call older people 'aunty' or 'uncle'. These are terms of affection and respect that acknowledge the aunty or uncle's seniority. I took some time to adjust to strangers being referred to as 'aunty' and 'uncle' as these terms are only used for family members in Australia, but I've now adopted the practice. It seems much nicer to tell my kids to say 'thank you' to 'the bus uncle' rather than 'the driver'.

People of a higher occupational rank are also automatically given great respect in Singapore. Students show great respect to their teachers, with the Singaporean student/teacher relationship much more formal than what is found in many Western countries these days. Even Singaporeans who are older than many of today's government ministers will only ever talk about the ministers in a respectful manner. Similarly, in the workplace Singaporeans will always be respectful and cordial to those people higher up the ladder and will rarely openly question the work decisions of a more senior colleague.

## Conservative

Singaporeans are by-and-large much more conservative than countries in the West. This means that generally they dress more conservatively, speak relatively quietly, express opinions less forcefully and have more conservative views.

In general I would say that Singaporeans flash far less flesh than many other places in the world, although expats won't usually need to change the way they dress to fit into Singapore. Singapore's 'dress code' may lean towards being conservative but at the same time it's also accommodating. However, if you enjoy being a nudist you will need to cover up as public nudity is illegal.

I've found that Singaporeans are not as loud, particularly in a group situation, as people from my home country. And as far as I can tell (although I understand only English) they curse in public a lot less! This is something that I really enjoy about Singapore and makes crowded public spaces far more pleasant than they would otherwise be.

## Etiquette

Whilst Singapore is fairly accommodating and accepting of the etiquette faux pas of foreigners there are a few easy to follow tips that will set you on the right path.

- Shoes should always be removed before entering a home. This is not only for cleanliness reasons but also because shoes are believed to bring bad luck into the house.

- Never touch someone's head as the head is considered sacred.

- Not all ethnicities are comfortable with body contact, including shaking hands. The easiest way to deal with this is to wait until the person you are meeting extends their hand. Kissing on the cheek or hugging as a greeting or a farewell is not generally done.

- When being introduced to someone smiling and nodding is acceptable. Kissing and hugging are not usual.

- The eldest in a group is usually introduced first. This shows respect for elders and is an important aspect of Singaporean society.

- Speak at a low volume. Yelling or talking loudly is considered rude.

- Pointing is usually done with a thumb, not a finger as this is considered bad manners.

- Do not serve pork products or alcohol to Muslims. Other meat products should be halal certified.

- Hindus do not eat beef and some are vegetarians.

- Use two hands (or extend one hand while touching your elbow with the other hand) when giving cash or credit cards.

Singaporeans are, for the most part, reasonably conservative with their values. Many topics discussed openly in Western countries are only discussed behind closed doors. For example, many countries have sanctioned same-sex marriage but Singapore has yet to start that particular conversation. Indeed, male-to-male homosexual sex is still illegal, despite rare prosecutions. Relocating from a place where issues like this are freely debated and discussed, to a country that is more restrained with the expression of personal opinions, can take some adjusting to. I have startled more than one Singaporean friend with my opinions and now tend to only weigh in if they raise a particular issue.

However, I have also found that many questions or remarks that are considered inappropriate elsewhere aren't here. It's not uncommon to be asked how much your rent is, how much you earn or to be told by a shopkeeper that there's no way your feet will fit in the shoes they sell (true story!). Whilst these questions and remarks may seem intrusive or insensitive, you should keep in mind that no malice is intended and the person is actually showing an interest in you. How you answer is entirely up to you, but one of the best ways to keep your culture shock in check is to try to not take offence at everything that is different, but to just accept it for what it is and move on. This is really hard at the start but I promise that it does get easier with time and practice!

### Calling Names

I'm embarrassed to admit that it took four years and writing this book to realise why I am called 'Ms Kelly' here, rather than 'Ms Jackson-Nash'. I didn't mind Ms Kelly as it seemed casual and cute, but it was the opposite of how I would have been formally addressed in my home country. As discussed in 'Chapter 3: People', there are lots of different naming conventions in Singapore. The Chinese traditionally place the family name before the given name; Malays often don't have a family name at all and neither do some Indians. This is why the standard way of formally addressing someone is Mr/Ms and the first part of their written name. I am Ms Kelly, whilst someone called Yusuf bin Iskender will be Mr Yusuf.

## CUSTOMS AND TRADITIONS

Three of the biggest events in life are undoubtedly births, marriages and deaths. Every culture in the world has their own traditions and rituals, and Singaporeans are no different. Whilst each of the three main ethnicities has distinct rituals and traditions that have been formed over centuries, they must still meet the legal requirements outlined in the law.

## Getting Married

Marriages in Singapore must all be registered with either the Registry of Marriages (ROM), or with the Registry of Muslim Marriages (ROMM) if the couple are Muslim. Marriage is legal for people over the age of 18, but those aged 18 to 21 will require a parent or legal guardian to give consent for the marriage. If both parties are aged 18 to 21 they will both need to attend a marriage preparation programme.

The first legal step taken is to make an appointment with ROM or ROMM to verify the documents and sign the statutory declaration. The next step is to file a Notice of Marriage online. If either or both of the couple aren't Singapore citizens or permanent residents, then they must be physically present in Singapore for 15 days prior to the lodgement of the Notice of Marriage. At this time the couple will need to provide information about themselves as well as their two witnesses. This information will be printed on the Certificate of Marriage.

The marriage solemnization (or ceremony) must take place between 21 days and three months of lodgement of the Notice of Marriage. The solemnisation (or ceremony) can take place at the ROM, ROMM or another venue provided an official solemniser officiates.

As there is a reasonable amount of paperwork involved in getting married in Singapore, some couples choose to have the solemnisation at the ROM/ROMM and then conduct a more traditional wedding ceremony separately.

## Having a Baby

Once a pregnancy is confirmed, most people will choose a doctor and/or a hospital. This decision is usually driven by the level of health cover held by the mum-to-be. Singapore has an excellent health system but without insurance the

BABY

PAPERWORK

TRIGG.

costs can mount up very quickly. After the baby is born, a Notification of Live Birth will be issued by the hospital. Within 14 days, at least one of the baby's parents must register the birth with either the Registry of Births and Deaths or at the registry office within the hospital. The person who registers the birth will need to take with them the Notification of Live Birth, both parents' identification documents (identity card (IC) and passport), and the parents' marriage certificate (if applicable). The baby's name will also be recorded at this stage. The birth certificate will be issued on the spot.

It's important to note that babies of expats born in Singapore do not automatically become Singapore citizens. Along with the Notification of Live Birth, expat parents will also be given an advisory note which entitles the baby to a Special

Pass that is valid for six weeks. Within this timeframe, expat parents will need to apply for a passport from their home country. As the process differs between countries, expats will need to contact their embassy or consulate to find out how to register the baby's birth and obtain a passport. Once the baby's passport is in hand, the parents can then apply to MOM for a Dependant Pass for the baby.

## Burial or Cremation?

On an island as small as Singapore, the issue of what to do with the remains of the deceased has been a continual problem. In colonial times, burial was the favoured method of dealing with deceased remains and there were a number of cemeteries throughout the island. However, the problem of space for the living has created a continual need. As of 1974, these were all closed for burials, with only Choa Chu Kang cemetery in the north-west of Singapore open to burials. Cremation was encouraged (although this had always been the predominant choice of Hindus) and many of the old cemeteries have had their graves exhumed and the land used for other purposes. Part of Bukit Brown cemetery is currently being redeveloped into a road. Today most Singaporeans opt for cremation over burials. This is partly for practicality and also because there is a 15-year limit on burials, after which time the remains will be exhumed and cremated.

When a death occurs, a doctor is required to issue a Certificate of Cause of Death (COCD) stating the cause of death. If the cause of death cannot be determined, the death will be referred to the coroner. If a death occurs at home and a doctor cannot attend, then it is best to contact the police who will make alternative arrangements. Once the COCD has been issued then a funeral director can be engaged. Deaths in Singapore, regardless of citizenship, must be registered with Registry of Births and Deaths within 24 hours. If the death occurred at a private hospital or at home, provided a doctor attended, then registration can also take place at a Neighbourhood Police Centre. The person registering the death will need to attend the Registry and take with them the Certificate of Cause of Death issued by the doctor or hospital, and other identification documents such as IC or passport. If all is in order the Death Certificate will then be issued.

## CHINESE CUSTOMS

Of the three major ethnicities in Singapore, the Chinese are the most superstitious. As such, Chinese traditions incorporate lots of rituals dating back hundreds of years that are a mix of Chinese folklore, religion and the modern day.

### Pregnancy and birth

The Chinese have had a lengthy list of pregnancy do's and don'ts for centuries, and many of these transferred to the Singaporean Chinese community. These vary depending upon where in China the family is from, but many have fallen out of fashion in recent times. Some of these traditions include avoiding moving any furniture or using a hammer. There are also foods to eat and other foods to avoid.

After the baby is born a Chinese mother will usually observe a 30-day confinement period called *zuo yue*. She will stay at home and not receive any visitors while she recuperates. Baths and showers are not taken for the first 10 days and the hair isn't washed for the entire 30 days. There is a strong emphasis on high-energy and high-protein foods such as chicken, fish and eggs. Soups are also popular, as is red date tea. Massage and wraps are used to reduce the size of the midsection and regain post-pregnancy shape.

The end of the confinement period is considered to be the first birthday of the baby, and a celebration will be held. The baby is usually dressed in new clothes, which are often red. Taoists and Buddhists may light incense and give food offerings as a way of introducing the baby to their deceased ancestors. The baby's head may also be shaved. The family may often give out gifts to visitors. Eggs dyed red for good luck, pickled ginger, meat and cakes are common 'one month' gifts. It's also customary for visitors to give an *ang pow* (red packet) with money inside. How much to give is up to the giver and depends upon how close the relationship is, but somewhere in the $50-$100 region is usual.

## Weddings

Chinese weddings are typically lavish. They are a way of displaying the families' wealth and prosperity, and if the wedding isn't considered up to scratch the family will lose face within the community. In modern Singapore, the outward appearance of a Chinese wedding is very similar to a Western wedding: white dress, suits, chauffeur-driven cars, multi-tiered wedding cake, professional photographer, and a reception at a fancy restaurant or hotel. However, underneath this veneer are many traditional Chinese customs. Each dialect group have their own set of customs but they often include gift giving and displays of filial piety.

On the day of the wedding, the traditional tea ceremony is held. This is the traditional way the two families are formally introduced. The bride and groom show filial piety by serving tea to their elders, which is also a way of welcoming the new member into each family. The bride and groom attend tea ceremonies at each of their families' houses, where as a couple they serve tea to their families in order of importance. This means that the eldest relatives are served first, and so on down the family tree.

The wedding banquet or buffet is held in the evening. Generally a wedding banquet is a relatively formal affair with lots of food courses and no dancing. The married couple move around the tables throughout the night to mingle with their guests. Guests will usually leave after the last course has been cleared. Some couples will opt for a less formal buffet which allows the guests to join in with karaoke or other entertainment that may be organised.

Gift-giving at Chinese weddings is usually money (an even amount) inside an *ang pow* (red packet). How much to give is usually based on the timing and location of the ceremony. Evening celebrations in a five-star hotel will require a bigger ang pow than a lunchtime event in a restaurant. The amount to give is so fraught with angst that there is now a website (www.weddingangbao.com) that provides a monetary guide based on time and location!

## Funerals

Unlike Malay and Hindu funerals which are conducted soon after death and are relatively low-key events, Chinese funerals can last between three and seven days. In Chinese customs, providing a decent funeral is seen as an important act of filial piety. Death is also seen as a transition, not an ending, and many of the funerary traditions are designed to make this transition smoother. A funeral wake is held before the funeral ceremony and this may take place at home, the void deck of an HDB flat or a funeral home.

Before the wake is held, the body of the deceased will

be washed and dressed. This is usually performed by the deceased's eldest son (if they have one) and the body will be wiped three times before being dressed. Some personal items of the deceased will be placed in the coffin with the body to accompany it to the netherworld. Food offerings will also be made, as well as joss sticks and paper money. These rituals signify the continuing relationship between the living and the deceased for Chinese people for whom ancestor worship is a very important part of their belief system.

The family members of the deceased will dress in sombre colours and wear a mourning pin (*xiao*) on their upper arm (left arm for men, right arm for women), which fastens a coloured piece of cloth to the shirt sleeve. This colour identifies their relationship to the deceased. The Chinese believe that it's good luck to have many visitors at a funeral wake, so mourners are welcome at any time throughout the day, although most will come in the evening. Visitors should stand at the foot of the coffin (which is usually open) and bow three times. If a mourner is either Taoist or Buddhist they may hold a burning joss stick while bowing. A family member will usually be kneeling nearby to burn joss sticks and paper money.

The family may present each mourner with a red string for their wrist (some families may place a bowl of red strings on the table for mourners to take), which is thought to ward off the spirits which are believed to gather at funerals. Custom dictates that mourners will remove it on the way home and throw it away. The spirits will follow the string and you won't be visited by spirits at your home. The family will usually offer mourners refreshments whilst condolences are given. When mourners leave the wake, they should not say goodbye to the family or shake hands.

The burial or cremation will usually take place on the third, fifth or seventh day after death. On the night before the burial or cremation, funeral rituals will be performed according to the family's religious beliefs. These prayers are an important ritual as they are thought to guide the deceased's journey to the netherworld and transform them from a ghost to an ancestor. On the day of the funeral ceremony, the family will walk behind the hearse for a short while before boarding a bus or a van to get to the crematorium or cemetery. Mourners are welcome to walk behind the family. The prayers and rituals performed as part of the funeral vary, depending on the family's religious practices. Buddhists and Taoists will usually ask a priest to perform chants, while Christians may offer prayers throughout the funeral period. If the family has opted for cremation, the family will return to the crematorium the next day and using chopsticks they will place the bones into an urn. The urn is either installed in a columbarium, at a temple, or taken home and placed on the ancestral altar. Traditionally Chinese people had an ancestral altar in their house which housed the urns of their ancestors remains, but in recent times many use a temple for this purpose.

It is customary to give money to the family to help with the funeral costs. This should be placed inside a white envelope and given to a senior member of the family. Floral wreaths are also acceptable to give during times of mourning. Rather than accepting cash or flowers many Chinese families now request a donation to a charity instead. If in doubt, it may be better to ask the family what they prefer.

The mourning period varies between families. Anywhere from a month to a year is common, although some families adhere to mourning dress only for the funeral period. Family members will wear dark-coloured clothes (no red, yellow or orange) and pin a small square of cloth to their sleeve as a sign of respect for the deceased. It's also common for Chinese to burn paper goods that will help make the deceased more comfortable in the netherworld. These paper items can be money, cars, houses, mobile phones, and any other thing you can possibly imagine! Buddhists will make offerings and say prayers for their deceased ancestors on the 7th and 49th days after their death, as well as on their birthdays.

## MALAY CUSTOMS
### Pregnancy and birth
In modern-day Singapore many of the traditional Malay pregnancy rituals are rarely carried out. Some, such as the *lenggang perut* (sway the belly), which occurs around the seventh month of pregnancy and is designed to move the baby from a breech position, are occasionally carried out at the wish of an older relative.

When a baby has been born and the umbilical cord has been cut, it's customary for the father to whisper the *azan* (call to prayer) into the baby's ear: the right ear for a boy and the left ear for a girl. This declares that the baby is a Muslim. Shortly after birth, one of the parents will touch the baby's lips with something sweet, such as honey, juice or dates. *Aqiqah*, which involves the slaughter of two animals for a male baby and one animal for a baby girl, is a long-standing Islamic tradition. It's not compulsory and only occurs if it's within the family's financial means. Some Singaporean Malays will send money to family in other countries to carry out this ritual instead.

Most Malay mums will observe a 44-day confinement period after they have a baby, called *dalam patang*. During this time the new mum will eat a restricted diet that includes avoiding 'cooling' foods such as cucumbers and cabbage as well as spicy food. Post-natal massage is believed to help eliminate wind from the body and lift the uterus back to its correct position. Abdominal binding (*barut*) and wrapping (*bengkung*) are commonplace and designed to help get the body back into its pre-pregnancy shape. At the end of the confinement period a Malay mother will bathe in lime juice and water as a way of cleansing her body of bad influences.

Traditionally Malay babies have their hair shaved seven days after birth, but this has gradually stretched out to within 40 days of the birth. The hair is weighed and then the equivalent amount in gold is donated by the father to the poor. A naming ceremony is usually held at the same time.

If you are visiting a Malay family who has welcomed a newborn baby then it's customary to give a gift of 'warming' foods for the mother. A gift for the baby is also customary.

## Marriage

Malay marriages are festive, colourful, joyous and noisy! The bride and groom are treated like a King and Queen and even have a throne to sit on. Malay weddings have two parts. The first is the formal solemnisation of the marriage in accordance with Islamic law called *nikah*. This is the official part of the wedding, where the marriage contract is signed, duties and obligations are discussed, and the groom places a ring on his wife's finger. The *nikah* usually, but not always, happens the day before the wedding celebration.

The second part of a Malay wedding is the *bersanding*. This begins when the bride sends someone to the groom's house saying she is ready to meet him. The groom will then

This Malay bridal couple pose on the *pelamin* (raised platform) during the *bersanding* ceremony. The bride is usually elaborately made up (notice the henna on her hands) and may have a few changes of costumes.

head to the bride's place, and there's a bit of playacting with the bridesmaids trying to prevent the groom from reaching the bride. The couple will be treated as a King and Queen for the day, and will sit together on a throne on the *pelamin* (dias). Relatives and friends will sprinkle the couple with various fertility offerings such as flower petals and yellow rice.

Malays take great pride in having a strong sense of community and the *walimah* (wedding feast) epitomises this. The guest list for a Malay wedding is usually large, but the celebrations are usually informal with guests not obligated to stay for the entire time. It's quite OK to drop by any time and stay for as long or as little as the guest is able. In the old days guests would bring a dish to be shared but most Malay weddings now have catering.

The dress code for a Malay wedding is usually 'smart casual', which means that collars and ties aren't required, but wear something smarter than shorts and t-shirts! Whilst there are no strict dress rules you should be respectful that dressing modestly is important in Islamic culture. Before you leave the wedding you should *salaam* (bow with hands touching your forehead) the bride and groom's parents and discreetly slip them a folded envelope of money. This is in place of a gift and the usual amount is about $20, but a greater amount is always welcome!

## Death

In accordance with Islamic tradition, burials for most Malays will take place within 24 hours of death. The body is usually washed by family and friends of the same gender as the deceased, although sometimes the spouse will attend to the washing. The body is then shrouded in a *kafan*, which are pieces of white cloth. Next, the cloth is dabbed with some non-alcoholic perfumes, camphor and powdered sandalwood.

Islamic funerals are solemn and dignified. A *jenazah* prayer is said by the attendees at the funeral. Whilst weeping is permitted, loud expressions of grief are frowned upon. After the *jenazah* prayer the body will be transported to Choa Chu Kang Muslim cemetery in a coffin. At the cemetery, the shrouded body will be removed from the coffin and placed into the earth on the right side with the head facing Mecca. The head covering is loosened so the skin of the cheek touches the ground. The grave will then be filled. Although in some Islamic cultures women are forbidden from attending burials, in Singapore women do attend the burial.

Non-Muslims may attend Muslim funerals and they should wear white or other sombre colours. However, it is customary that only family and very close friends attend Muslim funerals, so it may be more appropriate to visit the family after the burial. Dark colours are usually worn as a sign of mourning, or an *abaya* if you are Malay. Flowers are usually not given to the family, and mourners will usually only stay a short time. "*Salam Takziah*" is the appropriate phrase to say to the family which means 'my condolences'.

The family will hold a *tahlil* or *kenduri* (thanksgiving commemoration) on the 3rd, 7th, 40th and 100th days after the burial. Islamic widows cannot remarry for a period of 4 months and 10 days after the death of their husband. This period of time is called *iddah* and the widow will also normally be dressed more modestly by not wearing jewellery or fashion accessories during this time.

## INDIAN CUSTOMS

Compared to the Malay community, the Indian community in Singapore is much more diverse. Religion, caste and heritage are all major influences on the way Indian family celebrate and commemorate the big events of life, and with such a wide range within the Indian community it's impossible to cover all the different traditions. As Hinduism is the most popular religion, this section will primarily focus upon the pregnancy, birth, wedding and death rituals of Hindus. However, even amongst Hindus there is a wide range of different traditions that stem from the different castes as well as the different places on the Indian subcontinent that Singaporean Indians draw their heritage from.

### Pregnancy and birth

Many of the traditional Indian pregnancy rituals have fallen out of fashion in Singapore. Some pregnant women may wear charms to ward off bad luck. At the third month of pregnancy, some may perform the *punsavana* ceremony which is performed to make the baby develop into a strong person. Toward the end of the pregnancy, there may be a kind of baby shower called a *simantonnyana*, where the mum-to-be is given gifts, as prayers are performed for the health of her and the baby. About 28 days after birth, the baby's head will be shaved as a way of giving thanks. Baby girls may also have their ears pierced at about the same time.

A confinement period of 30 to 40 days is observed by most new Indian mothers. During this time, certain foods (cooling foods such as cucumbers and tomatoes) are avoided, a diet aimed to avoid wind is followed, physical exertion and housework is kept to a minimum, a warm daily bath is taken although showers are avoided, and both mother and baby

will enjoy oil massages. Tummy binding using a sari is also a common practice.

## Marriage

India has a long tradition of arranged marriages, and even though the Singaporean Indian community has moved increasingly toward 'love' marriages there are still some that opt for an arranged marriage. The format of Indian weddings in Singapore varies widely, which reflects the breadth of different backgrounds of the Indian community. However, there are a few traditions which can be found in most Indian weddings. The first ceremony before the wedding day is the Bangle Ceremony, where the groom will visit the bride's home and present her with bangles. She will also have her hands and feet decorated with henna at this time. The belief is that the darker the henna the deeper the bride's love for the groom! The next important ritual is the smelting of gold for the *thali*, which is a small golden pendant that serves the same purpose as a wedding ring. After this ceremony the couple do not see each other until the wedding day.

On the day of the wedding ceremony the groom arrives at the temple first and he has a piece of cord around his finger. When the bride arrives, her father performs the *kanyadaan*, which is essentially passing her care from father to husband and also acknowledging the bride's purity. The bride and groom will then sit side-by-side and the rest of the ceremony will include the tying of cord to the bride's finger which unites her with her groom and the blessing of her *sari* and *thali*. At this point the bride will move to another room to change into her wedding sari. When she returns the groom will tie the *thali* around her neck. Saffron rice and flower petals are then thrown to celebrate the marriage and bless the marriage.

The final part of the ceremony is when the bride and groom walk three times around the ceremonial fire and afterwards the groom puts toe-rings on the bride's toes.

Indian weddings are colourful, joyous and traditional, and the clothing of the guests reflects this. Women typically wear a colourful *sari*. Gifts of money or jewellery are acceptable.

### Death

Hindu funerals typically take place at home and cremation usually takes place within 24 hours of death. A Hindu priest and senior members of the person's family will perform the funeral rituals and chants. After death, the body is bathed and dressed in a clean set of clothes, before being placed in a casket that will stay open for mourners to say farewell. The deceased will be garlanded with flowers, and oil lamps will be lit throughout the room. After the rituals are complete, the casket will be transferred to the hearse and travel to either the crematorium or the cemetery.

It's a common belief that all Hindus are cremated, but this is not the case. Tamil Hindus have traditionally favoured burial and Hindu children are also buried. Choa Chu Kang Cemetery has a Hindu burial section for those choosing burial over cremation. However, in modern Singapore, with the 15-year timeframe on burials, most Hindus today favour cremation.

Non-Hindus are welcome to attend Hindu funerals. It is traditional to wear white or other sombre colours, but black is considered inappropriate. Casual clothes are favoured over more formal attire. Flowers are welcome, but it's not necessary to offer food to the relatives of the deceased. Ten days after the death, some families will hold a ceremony that helps the deceased's spirit ascend to heaven. Attendees at this ceremony will usually take a gift of fruit.

# CHAPTER 5

# PRACTICALITIES

*Move to a new country and you quickly see that visiting a place as a tourist, and actually moving there for good, are two very different things.*

**— Tahir Shah, Travels With Myself**

In the months before you depart for Singapore, you will spend a great deal of dismantling all the infrastructure of your life. You will spend countless hours sorting and culling your possessions, disconnecting utilities, writing lists and crossing them off, selling your car and the like as you prepare to leave one country for another. It's always a good idea to enjoy the flight(s) between countries as much as you possibly can; once you arrive in Singapore, it's time to reconstruct everything that you've just dismantled, except now you get to do it in a new system with companies that probably won't work exactly the same way they did back 'home'. Many companies will provide their expatriate employees with a relocation company or agent who will help you build the framework of your new life in Singapore, but just as many people will have to navigate this on their own. The logistics of juggling all of these different decisions and responsibilities can test your patience to breaking point but a bit of forward planning and helpful tips can smooth the path.

## WORK PASSES AND PERMITS

Before you can begin work, or do any of the important bits of reconstructing your life in Singapore, you will need to have the appropriate work permit and dependant passes (if applicable). As it's usual for most companies to handle this part of the relocation process for their expat employees, I've provided only a summary of the most applicable passes.

- **Employment Pass (EP):** Professionals arriving in Singapore as part of a company-sponsored relocation will usually receive a work permit known as an EP, provided they meet the salary and qualification standards. EP pass-holders are eligible to receive Dependant's Passes (DP) for their dependants.

- **Personalised Employment Pass (PEP):** High-earning professionals who aren't sponsored by a company can apply for a PEP. PEP pass-holders are eligible to receive DPs for their dependants.

- **EntrePas:** Foreign entrepreneurs looking at starting a business in Singapore can apply an EntrePass. EntrePass holders are not eligible to apply for DPs for their family until they renew their pass and meet an additional set of requirements.

- **S Pass:** This is for mid-level skilled staff earning more than $2,200 per month, with relevant qualifications and work experience.

- **Training Employment Pass:** This is for foreign workers who are coming to Singapore to undertake professional training. They must earn more than $3,000 per month.

- **Work Holiday Programme:** This is for people aged 18–25 who are moving to Singapore to work and holiday for a period up to six months in length.

- **Training Work Permit:** This is for semi-skilled

For more detailed information on all passes you should visit the Ministry of Manpower (MOM) website (www.mom.gov.sg/passes-and-permits). The requirements for all of the passes change from time to time so if you have to sort this out yourself, make sure you check the website for the latest updates.

trainees or students who are moving to Singapore to undertake practical training up to six months in length.

## Other Passes

- **Dependant's Pass:** For those holding an EP, PEP or S Pass, their legally married spouse and children can be issued with a Dependant's Pass (DP) each. It is possible for people on a DP to work in Singapore but your employer will need to arrange for a Letter of Consent (LOC) from the Ministry of Manpower.
- **Long Term Visit Pass:** This may be issued for parents, common-law spouses or step-children of EP or S Pass holders. People on a LTVP will need to get a work pass to work in Singapore unless they are married to either a Singapore citizen or Permanent Resident (PR).

## Documents Required

Your employer will usually apply for your work permit online and provide all of the documentation pertaining to the company but you will still need to provide documentation, so make sure you have access to the following:

- Passports
- Academic transcripts
- Marriage certificate
- Birth certificates for biological children
- Adoption orders for adopted children
- Two passport photos of each applicant

You should receive an 'In-Principle Approval' letter confirming that you have been granted a work permit before you move to Singapore, which you can present at Immigration on arrival. In the first few days after arrival you will need to attend an interview at MOM where they will make sure that all of your paperwork is in order and also take your thumbprint, which will be printed on your employment or dependant's pass. If you don't already have passport photos, there is a photo kiosk just outside of the MOM building. It will take a few days for your identification card (IC) to be printed. When it is ready you can collect them yourself or your company may arrange for it to be delivered. Your IC is the size of a credit card and lists your personal details, the type of pass, your identification number and your thumb print.

## REMOVALISTS

When considering any international move, always get several quotes from reputable moving companies. Entrusting all of your worldly goods to an unproven company may save you money in the short-term but create a lot of pain in the long-term. As with all products and services, prices will vary so make sure you get a few quotes and also ask the company what they do and don't do as not all movers are equal. In order to meet customs and insurance requirements you will not be allowed to pack your own boxes.

Do check with the company as to whether they will be unpacking your goods in Singapore or just delivering the boxes and furniture. (Do note that 'unpacking' will not mean placing your things into cupboards but just entails taking them out of the boxes.) They should also give you a list of what you can and can't pack in the shipment and which goods have duty or declarations needed. For example, as pornography is illegal you will likely have to supply a list of videos or DVDs you plan to bring with you, and if Singapore customs are concerned about their subject matter you may have to pay

for them to be viewed and approved by the government. On top of Singapore's requirements each individual company will also have their own requirements.

## WHAT TO BRING

'What should I bring?' is a common refrain from soon-to-be expats and not as easy to answer as it sounds. Singapore is a modern, well-equipped city and you can buy almost anything here, albeit at prices that may be considerably different than from your previous location, so if you decide to just arrive with a couple of suitcases you'll be able to buy everything you need when you arrive. Before you plan on what you should bring, check the employment contract and how much shipping it includes, if any. Employment contracts vary wildly so check it thoroughly to make sure you know exactly what you are entitled to before you get carried away stockpiling groceries in your home country to ship to Singapore. Some contracts include a small air shipment, others a sea container and others just what you can pack into your plane luggage allowance.

## To pack or not to pack?

Prohibited Goods—ie. do not bring under any circumstances
- Chewing gum (except approved oral dental and medicated gum by HSA)
- Chewing tobacco and imitation tobacco products (e.g. electronic cigarettes, etc)
- Cigarette lighters of pistol or revolver shape
- Controlled drugs and psychotropic substances
- Endangered species of wildlife and their by-products
- Firecrackers
- Obscene articles, publications, video tapes/discs and software
- Reproduction of copyright publications, video tapes, video compact discs, laser discs, records or cassettes
- Seditious and treasonable materials

Controlled Goods—paperwork involved (and possible fees)
- Animals, birds and their by-products; endangered species of wildlife and their by-products;
- Meat, fish, seafood, fruits and vegetables;
- Arms, explosives and weapons of any sort;
- Films, videos, video games, audio records;
- Pharmaceuticals, medicines and poisons;
- Telecommunication and radio communication equipment such as walky-talkies;
- Radioactive material and apparatus.

Dutiable goods—fees involved
- Alcoholic products
- Tobacco products
- Motor vehicles
- Petrol products

What to bring really gets down to personal preference but some things to think about include:

- Condo apartments can be quite small and staircases can be narrow, so think about the size of your furniture and whether it will fit in your potential new home. If in doubt, leave it behind as it will save you the trouble of trying to store or sell it in Singapore.
- Large electrical appliances such as fridges, washers and dryers, are usually included in rental properties so don't bring them. Singapore runs on 240 voltage so if your appliances work on a different voltage then you should either leave them behind or purchase a transformer to plug them into.
- The humidity is not great for paper goods like precious books, documents and photographs.
- Any other rules/guidelines stipulated by your moving company.

### Bringing Your Pet

It is possible to relocate your pet(s) to Singapore, so long as they are cats or dogs and not one of the banned breeds, but it will come with a rather hefty price tag. Friends of mine who brought their pets with them spent between $2,000 and $10,000 relocating them. You will need to comply with all Singaporean legislation, which involves getting an import licence from the Agri-food and Veterinary Authority (AVA), an International Health Certificate from an approved veterinarian, Vaccination Certificates and an ISO-compatible micro-chip. The procedure for relocating pets differs depending upon the country of origin and the AVA website has detailed information on this at www.ava.gov.sg. There are many pet relocation companies worldwide who will help you move your pet to

Singapore. A word of caution: if your pet contracts tick fever during its stay in Singapore some countries will not allow the pet to relocate there, so you may have to rehome it.

## SOMEWHERE TO LIVE

The decision as to which part of Singapore to live in is one of the uppermost concerns in most people's minds. It's inordinately difficult to decide upon an area to live when you've not spent a great deal (if any) time in the country. However, the bonus of being a small island is that you're never too far from anywhere. When deciding where to live you should consider your lifestyle and what is important to you and your family. Some of the factors to consider are proximity to transport, work and schools. Each person or family will have their own unique requirements and it's important to think about these in advance so that your real estate agent can

match your needs with properties. For example, proximity to a park or the coast might be important to families while those without kids in tow might prefer a location closer to restaurants and nightlife.

## Things to Consider
### To rent or to buy?

The vast majority of people moving to Singapore for work choose to rent a property rather than buy. It is possible for non-Singaporeans to buy property to live in and for investment purposes, but they are restricted mainly to condominiums. Other properties require approval from the government. The Singapore Land Authority (SLA) website has more information on this at www.sla.gov.sg.

### Budget

It's a good idea before you get too far into researching areas to live and looking at individual properties that you know what

sort of budget you have. If you have a company-allocated housing budget then check with the company, but if you will be allocating your own housing budget then sit down and crunch some numbers so that you're not looking at properties above what you can afford. This will save you disappointment and time further down the road. Singapore rents are notoriously high so be prepared for your jaw to drop when you check out some of the online property sites. The rental market is largely driven by the expatriate market as most are only in Singapore for a short period of time, so rents rise and fall in accordance with their demand for property. Catching the market in a downswing, when rents are falling and you have good bargaining power, is really nothing more than luck as most people moving do not have the luxury of waiting until the market is favourable. This also means that when your lease is up for renewal that the asking price could fall significantly, but conversely if the market is on the way up then you may well be asked to pay a lot more than you do currently.

Another quirk of the rental market in Singapore is that some landlords do not lower rents in response to the lowering of the market. Even though every other property in the development is asking a lower price they will refuse your fair offer and let the property stand vacant for extended periods rather than losing face. If you encounter this situation then there is nothing you can do but move on to other properties!

## Location

Settling on a location to live in is an incredibly hard thing when you've never lived in Singapore before, a little akin to throwing a dart at the map and hoping it all works out OK! A good place to start is to take a map and mark the places where you and your family will be spending a lot of time (work and school) and work from there. Easy access to an MRT station or a direct bus line will save you hours in commuting time, although this may be less important if you're planning to get a car. If you have children also check with the school about bus arrangements and how long the journey typically is for various areas. Choosing a property closer to your children's school will save them a bus or car journey but do factor in the Singapore climate and what would be a comfortable walk in your home country will more than likely be a hot and sweaty one here. There's also tropical downpours to contend with. Lastly, check the map for nearby supermarkets and malls. Having a supermarket within easy walking distance is particularly important if you're not planning on getting a car, although online grocery shopping has helped enormously in this area.

## Size

Singapore apartments and houses are usually low on storage space so it's always a good idea to go for the biggest space you can find within your budget. Floor space can vary even within the same condo so keep looking until you find an apartment with the right amount of space for you. As a general guide, older condos will often have larger rooms than newer condos, so try to look past the sleek appearance of newer builds and think practically about your decision. Two years is a long time to be tied to a property that you find too small. When considering the space, check with your agent what it includes. Is it just the indoor space? Does it include outdoor area like a terrace or the car park space?

Property sizes in Singapore are usually in square metres, not square feet.

Properties are usually marketed using the number of bedrooms they have and you'll then often see a '+1' (for example, 3+1) and this indicates that there is an extra room (usually a VERY small room) for a domestic worker. If you're considering employing a domestic worker during your time in Singapore, then making sure you have the space for her is crucial. Whilst apartments might lack built-in storage units, they usually have a number of bathrooms, with many newly built properties having an ensuite to every bedroom!

## Facilities and Amenities

The facilities and amenities provided at condos vary wildly from one to another. Older condos tend to provide less, although most have a pool, but newer condos often come with a dizzying array of facilities. Alongside the standard pool, gym and barbecue pits there are reflexology paths, meditation decks, cigar rooms, yoga rooms, and the like. Whilst you may be dazzled with all the facilities consider how often you will use them. A steam room or sauna may seem a very tempting treat but given the amount you will sweat in your day-to-day living in Singapore it may not be such a useful facility!

## Fixtures and Fittings

Properties are usually advertised as being partially or fully furnished. Fully furnished is self-explanatory and a good option if you will only be in Singapore for a short while or if your budget doesn't cover the shipping costs of all of your household goods. A partially furnished property rarely includes any actual furniture, but rather includes a fridge, a washing machine, a dryer and, occasionally, a dishwasher.

Another quirk of the Singapore rental market is that kitchens may not come with hot water to the tap or a built-in oven. If these things are important to you, do not let their absence deter you from the property as you can ask the landlord for these to be included.

Consider the age and condition of the air conditioners, as newer units tend to run more efficiently, which will help reduce your power bills. Ask the landlord how old the units are and also ask when they were last chemically cleaned. If they haven't been chemically cleaned in the last year then ask to have this done before you sign the lease. If you're not keen on running the air-conditioning then make sure you look to see if ceiling fans have been installed, or request that they are if you would like them.

## Safety

It is particularly important, if you have children, to take into account whether windows and balconies are fitted with safety barriers, grills, bars or other safety devices as there is no law that mandates window and balcony safety requirements, even on the highest buildings. If there are no safety features fitted, ask the landlord to fit them, or be prepared to pay to have them fitted yourself. If they aren't fitted then ask your agent whether the condo's Management Committee (MC) allow these to be fitted, as some condos forbid the fitting of safety fixtures that are visible on the façade of the building in order to preserve its aesthetic appeal. Whilst this has been successfully challenged in court in favour of the tenant, if you encounter an MC who puts aesthetics ahead of safety then I would strongly recommend looking at other condos.

## Construction noise

Construction is never-ending in Singapore and living next to a construction site is not for everyone, so ensure you ask your

agent if there is any construction scheduled in the foreseeable future. You could also consider asking the condo security guards or other residents to be doubly sure. However, if you are willing to put up with construction noise you just may well get a bargain as many landlords will lower the rent if there is construction activity nearby.

## Vibe of the place

The ambiance of any property changes at different times of the day and week, so if possible revisit a property that you like several times before committing. This will give you a chance to see how the neighbourhood varies, as a condo that is quiet in the morning when all the occupants are at school and work can turn into a zoo after school hours and on the weekend! If you have kids and like a lively environment then this may work well for you, but if you don't have kids and prefer a quiet neighbourhood then you may be better off with another property. This also applies for road noise which can increase greatly during peak travel times.

Also visit the apartment you like at different times of the day as a west-facing one may be lovely and cool in the morning but turn into a furnace when the afternoon sun hits the windows. This will increase your electricity bills as you will run the air-conditioning more.

## Types of housing
### HDB flats

Flats built by the Housing Development Board (HDB) are where the majority of Singaporeans live, with over 95 per cent being owners, but HDB flats aren't just for locals. Foreigners are able to privately rent entire HDB flats that are owned by Singapore citizens. The owners are also able to let single bedrooms, which is a good option for single expats on a limited budget.

As of 2014 the government has placed a quota on the number of flats that can be leased to non-Singaporean and non-Malaysia citizens of 8 per cent in any one neighbourhood and 11 per cent in individual blocks. The reasoning behind this is to preserve the unique character of the HDB heartlands. Whilst the idea of quotas based upon ethnicity may seem an odd policy to those new to Singapore it has been a practice here since 1989 when the government introduced the Ethnic Integration Policy (EIP), which limits the percentage of flats owned or leased based upon ethnicity. These percentages are based upon the proportions of each ethnicity in the broader Singaporean population and aim to preserve racial harmony and to prevent the occurrence of ethnic enclaves.

HDB flats don't typically come with the facilities and amenities of condos, like pools and gyms, but they are usually conveniently located near to transport, shopping and dining options. The reduced cost of living and the chance to live within the local community make leasing a HDB flat an attractive option that many expats overlook when thinking of where to live.

If you're interested in what the inside of a HDB flat is like, but don't have any local friends to call upon, you can visit the HDB showflats at the HDB hub in Toa Payoh.

## Condominiums

Condominiums (condo) are the most popular choice for expats in Singapore. Condos range from relatively small (just a few storeys high), with basic facilities, to multi-tower skyscrapers with every conceivable facility and amenity, including meditation corners, concierge and reflexology paths in addition to the usual gym and pool. As you would expect, the more central the location, the better the view, the more bells and whistles—and the higher the rent!

The advantage of a condo over landed properties is the ready-made community, which can help to ease the transition into Singapore. Many condos arrange social activities that can help you meet people and even just hanging out by the pool can help you form new friendships. The downside is that you are living above, below and alongside other people which may be a new experience for many people new to apartment living.

Older condos typically have fewer facilities than newer condos, although most have a pool, but their advantage is that they typically have more floor space than new condos.

## Cluster House Condos

A cluster house condo is a cross between a condo and a landed property. Essentially it's a group of terrace houses joined together, each usually three or four storeys high, but with many of the facilities of a condo such as a pool and BBQ pits. They range anywhere from six units to over a hundred units in the complex. As with high-rise condos the larger the development, the more choice of facilities you have.

## Landed Houses

Landed properties have just as much variety as both condos and cluster houses. Some landed houses come with a large yard and others just a courtyard and a car space. Some are freestanding (detached), some share a common wall with the house next door (semi-detached) and others are terrace houses that share common walls with neighbours. Detached houses can be single or double-storey. Most are modern builds but there are also some built during colonial times that are full of character and typically painted white with black trim, which is why they are called 'Black and White houses'.

Each style of landed house comes with its own advantages and disadvantages. Houses usually have more floor space than condos, and also more outdoor space, which may provide many expats with a lifestyle similar to that of their home country.

One of the disadvantages is that leasing a landed house will probably cost you more than just the monthly rental month as you may well be responsible for garden maintenance, which includes gardening and mosquito fogging. Remember that gardens grow quickly in the tropics, so keeping the garden neat, tidy and mosquito-free is an ongoing cost. If the property has a pool/jacuzzi/lift then you should also check who is responsible for the maintenance and repairs.

## The Leasing Process

A unique aspect of the Singapore leasing process is that both the tenant and the landlord have their own, separate agent. This means that the process has four parties involved: the tenant, the tenant's agent, the landlord and the landlord's agent. Many companies supply their expatriate staff with a real estate agent, but if not then the best way to find a reputable agent is by asking colleagues or friends for recommendations.

Once you settle on a property to lease your agent will draft a Letter of Intent (LOI) and you will be asked to pay a Good Faith Deposit (usually equivalent of a month's rent). The LOI will outline your rental amount, the duration of the lease, and any repairs or additions you are requesting. It will also include a Diplomatic Clause, which can be invoked should you be relocated away from Singapore before the lease expires. A two-year lease typically has a Diplomatic Clause of 12 months, so that after the lease has been running for a year you can end the lease, should you need to relocate, by giving two months' notice.

If the landlord accepts the conditions outlined in the LOI then they will begin drawing up the Tenancy Agreement (TA). This is the legally binding lease contract, so ensure that you read it carefully before signing. Take note of these points

- Diplomatic Clause: this will state that after a period of time (typically 14 months for a two-year lease) you can end the lease without penalties should you be transferred away from Singapore.
- Utilities: the contract should state the utilities that

are connected and what you are financially responsible for.

- Repairs and maintenance: the contract should state what repairs and maintenance the tenant is liable for and will typically state that the tenant is responsible for the first $150 (sometimes more) of minor repairs. Should also stipulate minimum time frames for air-conditioning, pool, lift, and pest control maintenance.
- Stamp duty
- Term of lease: one or two years and with/without option to renew.

If you are moving into a condo you (or your removalist) will need to check with the condo's management to arrange a suitable time for the unloading of your container. Some condos will require a security deposit to cover any damage that may occur to common areas.

## Temporary Accommodation

After you arrive in Singapore there will most likely be a short period of time where you will have to find temporary accommodation whilst you either find a property to lease or buy, or if you've already sorted that out then while you await your shipping container. Fortunately, Singapore has a good choice of serviced apartments to suit a range of budgets located around the island, although most tend to be concentrated around the Orchard and central areas. Most serviced apartments only offer stays longer than seven days so if you

Singapore Serviced Apartments Association website is a good starting place to find temporary accommodation that suits your location and budget. www.servicedapartments.org.sg

require accommodation for a shorter time then a hotel will be more suitable. If you're moving to Singapore for less than a year then staying in a serviced apartment may well be a good idea and most are open to negotiating a cheaper rate for longer stays.

## SCHOOLS AND CHILD CARE

If you are moving to Singapore with children, choosing a school and arranging child care will be at the very top of your to-do list. Fortunately, Singapore is a child-friendly country that provides lots of options for both child care and for schooling.

### Child-care

As Singapore is not a cheap place to live it is usual in local families for both parents to work full-time, so there is a wide variety of child-care options for younger kids on offer. Most child-care centres will offer a structured kindergarten programme for children aged three to six, and there's a wide range of curriculum available. Whilst it's great news that you'll have a wide range of centres to choose from, the bad news is that you'll be ineligible for government-subsidised child care so will have to pay the full cost, which can run in excess of $2,000 per month for a full-time place.

For a list of all child-care centres in Singapore visit the Early Childhood Development Agency's website at https://www.childcarelink.gov.sg/ccls/home/CCLS_Home.jsp

When considering which centre to choose it's always wise to visit and speak to the teachers and management. Check how the children's days are structured, what sort of curriculum is followed, whether there is a bus, wait-list times and—of course—the fees payable.

## Schools

The decision as to which school your kids will attend in Singapore may be complicated by the plethora of schools and curriculums on offer. Besides the local school system there are roughly 40 international schools, which can make choosing a school a bewildering experience. Here are some things to think about when selecting a school:

- **School calendar:** The school calendar year varies from country to country. Broadly, the school year in the northern hemisphere runs from August until June, and in the southern hemisphere it runs from February to December. If you choose a school that operates on a different school year to your home country then your kids will either have to jump forward or jump back a grade. If you're intending to stay in Singapore for a long time this may not be a factor, but for a short stay it may be an easier transition to choose a school that runs on the same calendar year. Also consider when the school holidays/vacations are if it's important for you and your family to return to your home country at set times each year.

- **Language:** Given the wide variety of international school you may choose to send your kids to a school that teaches in your native language in order to make it an easier transition. However, many parents from non-English speaking backgrounds opt to enrol their kids in an English-speaking school in order to improve their English abilities. Both decisions have their merits.

- **Special needs:** Parents with special needs children should be aware that not all international schools have the relevant facilities and staff. Be upfront with any potential schools about your child's needs so that they can advise if the school is a good fit or suggest alternatives. International schools typically charge large application fees so it's best to know before you add your child to the wait list.

- **Budget:** The fees charged by international schools vary wildly. Currently, the yearly fees for elementary schools range from $16,000 to $32,000 and secondary schools range from $18,000 to $37,000. On top of the annual tuition fees you may also have to pay application fees, re-enrolment fees, infrastructure fees and technology fees. Excursion/ field trip and camp fees are also usually additional.

- **School and class sizes:** Many of the international schools are very large, both in terms of their campuses and the number of enrolled students with several over the 2,500-student mark. Whilst their class sizes may be relatively small a large campus does not suit every child so consider checking out smaller schools if you think this will suit your child better.

- **Extra-curricular activities:** What activities are on offer in regard to sport, music, charity? What are the costs involved? Are extra-curricular activities compulsory and do they cost extra?

- **Location:** A centrally located school will make it easier to find somewhere to live, particularly if the working parent is also working nearby. Don't just trust the address listed on the school's website, as schools do relocate from time to time, so ensure that you ask if there are any plans for the campus to move in the foreseeable future.

- **Curriculum:** Every school has a different approach to curriculum, with many offering a single approach such as International Baccalaureate (IB), GCSE or a combination of approaches.
- **Transport:** Does the school offer a bus service? Is there an additional bus service for after school activities? How much is the cost? Is there a supervisor (often called a 'bus *amah*') on the bus and are the buses trackable online? If your kids plan to ride a bike or scooter to school is there somewhere safe to store them during the school day?
- **Uniform:** Is a school uniform compulsory and, if so, how expensive is it?
- **Settling-in process:** Many people come to Singapore on a two- or three-year work contract so international schools have a relatively high student turnover. Most will work very hard at making sure that new students are made to feel welcome. Some will ask the kids to come in for a day before the start of the academic year to familiarise them with the school's layout and provide them with a student buddy during their first weeks on campus.
- **Wait list:** Many international schools have a wait list which is sometimes years long, so early in your enquiry process specifically ask about wait list times. There's no point deciding upon a school only to find there's a year-long wait list!
- **Admission requirements:** Not all schools have admission requirements but some require students to be proficient in a particular language or give priority to children of the school's nationality.
- **Facilities:** What facilities are there on campus?

## Local Schools

While the local school system may be very different from what you might have experienced in your home country, the Singaporean school system has received many global accolades, particularly for their mathematics and science curriculums. If you are intending to make Singapore your home for the long-term and would like to avoid high school fees, then checking out the local system is worthwhile. However, it's important to be aware that as expatriates you will be at the very bottom of the eligibility pile as both locals and permanent residents will be allocated school places ahead of you. As a result you may not be able to enrol your children in your local school of choice.

Formal schooling begins in Singapore in the year that a child turns 7 and they will begin in Primary One. Primary school lasts for six years and secondary school for four or five. At the end of Primary Six, the students take the Primary School Leaving Exam (PSLE), and the results of this exam determine which secondary school they can apply to. Secondary school students are streamed into one of the four courses: Special, Express, Normal (Academic) or Normal (Technical). Most schools offer the GCE O Level course, while a select few offer the IB programme.

If you are considering local schools for your children, then visit the Ministry of Education (MOE) website, which outlines the different admission processes which depend on your child's age and chosen school (www.moe.gov.sg/education/admissions/international-students).

## UTILITIES

Once you have signed your lease and have a move-in date then you will need to arrange for the utilities (electricity, water

and gas) to be connected. Singapore Power (SP) handles the billing of gas, electricity and water, so you just have to deal with one company. To arrange connection, visit the SP website (www.singaporepower.com.sg) and complete the application form, making sure you have the required documents such as Tenancy Agreement, IC number and security deposit. SP will typically arrange for connection of the electricity and water on the next working day after you have applied. The security deposit is $500 for condos and $800 for landed properties as of August 2016.

The supply of gas for cooking is either via City Gas (gas mains) or by gas bottle/cylinder. If your property is connected to City Gas then SP will handle the billing but after you have opened an account with them you will need to call City Gas and arrange for them to turn your gas supply on.

If the stove top uses bottled gas then you will firstly need to check if there is already a gas bottle on site. If there isn't you will need to call a gas provider to bring a new bottle and the best way to find someone who will install a gas bottle is to google 'Singapore bottled gas suppliers'. This may be a completely different process to what you are used to but service is generally quick so within 24 hours you should be cooking with gas.

## TELECOMMUNICATIONS

You only need to take a quick trip on public transport or take a short walk and observe the number of people peering at their mobile phones or tablets to realise that Singapore is a country obsessed with digital communications, so it should come as no surprise that getting and staying connected is relatively easy.

There are three major telecommunications companies—Starhub, Singtel and M1. A fourth, MyRepublic, was started in 2011. The three major companies offer prepaid and postpaid mobile phone plans, broadband internet, home phone and cable television plans, either individually or as a bundle. MyRepublic offers internet services only. All companies explain their services, bundles and pricing on their websites and you can call their customer service lines to arrange billing and connection.

- **Starhub:** www.starhub.com
- **Singtel:** www.singtel.com
- **M1:** www.m1.com.sg
- **MyRepublic:** www.myrepublic.com.sg

If you are keen to get a local mobile phone number as soon as you arrive in Singapore you can buy prepaid SIM cards at most convenience stores by presenting your passport and paying a fee. This is a good option while you're trying to choose which mobile telephone provider to sign with.

## Television, Radio and Print Media

If you decide against buying a cable television subscription then you can still tune into the eight free-to-air television channels provided by MediaCorp. There is an English news channel, a kids channel, as well as general channels broadcasting in the four official languages of Malay, Tamil, Mandarin and English. There are multiple radio channels broadcasting in Singapore that offer a range of different musical genres as well as languages.

The main daily newspaper is The Straits Times which covers local, regional and international news, as well as human interest, sport and business stories. It also has a subscription-based website.

## Postal Services

Singapore Post (SingPost) is the local postal service. Outlets are located around the island and their website lists all branches and services. If you just want to buy local or international stamps, you can buy them over the counter or use a Self Automated Machine (SAM). These are usually located outside of SingPost branches and save you waiting in a long line. SingPost also handles a number of other services including bill payment and online shopping.

Singapore postal boxes are white or silver and can be found at various locations around Singapore, including at many petrol/gasoline stations and outside shopping centres.

# TRANSPORT

## Public Transport

Unlike many densely-populated cities around the world Singapore is an easy city to get around. A lot of thought, planning and skill has gone into making sure that transport runs efficiently and effectively, and public transport delays are treated as very serious matters. After major delays on one MRT line in December 2011 a government investigation was conducted and a public apology was issued in The Straits Times newspaper. If this was standard practice in other cities there would be no place for any news in the newspapers! So, be reassured that Singapore takes providing an efficient, low-cost public transport system seriously and the results speak for themselves.

The first MRT line opened in 1987 and there are currently five MRT lines with three more in either the construction or planning stages. With a daily ridership of almost three million commuters the MRT is a clean, efficient and safe transport option.

## Mass Rapid Transport (MRT)

The MRT is Singapore's famed train system and the easiest way to get around if your departure and destination points are near MRT stations. The first MRT line opened in 1987 and the system has continually expanded, with expansion plans scheduled through until 2030. There are no timetables, but rather trains will arrive around every six minutes with more frequent services at peak times. Train operation hours are from 5.30 am to about midnight daily and are usually extended during festive periods.

## Light Rail Transit (LRT)

LRT networks are situated in some HDB estates and connect flats in the estates to the nearest MRT station.

## Buses

Singapore has an extensive bus network, with several major bus interchanges throughout the island. Travelling by bus is the cheapest way to travel. It also has the added advantage of being above ground so it may help you get your bearings when you first arrive. It's very rare these days for buses to not be air-conditioned but if you do happen across one then your fare will be lower than that for air-conditioned buses.

### Timetables

As mentioned, there are no timetables for the MRT but there are published timetables for all the scheduled bus services. The easiest way to work out how to get to your destination using public transport is by using either an website or application. These will show you all the various ways that you can get to your destination as well as estimating the fare. Some reliable apps or websites can be found at:
- www.gothere.sg
- www.mytransport.sg
- www.smrt.com.sg

## Ticketing

### Stored-value Cards

The easiest way to pay for your public transport fares is by stored-value cards, such as EZ Link or NETS FlashPay cards. These are reusable cards that can be purchased at Passenger Service Centres as well as at convenience stores island-wide for $12, with $7 credit included. When you enter or exit the MRT station or the bus you tap the card on the reader and the correct fare will be deducted from your balance. You won't be able to use the card for MRT travel if the balance is less than $4. Cards can be topped up at a wide variety of places including the machines in the MRT stations, Passenger Service Counters, ASX machines, ATMs and convenience stores. EZ Link and NETS FlashPay cards can also be used to pay for purchases at selected stores.

### Single Use Cards

If you don't have a stored-value card then you can buy a single or return ticket for the MRT/LRT from the machine at the station. You simply select where you are travelling from and to, pay the fare and the machine will issue you a ticket.

### Paying the Driver

If you're catching a bus you can also get a single-use ticket from the driver as you board. The fare will usually be between $1 and $2; deposit the coins in the cash box near the driver and a ticket will be printed. No change will be given.

### Children

Children under 0.90 cm and who haven't yet started elementary school can use all public transport for free by getting a Child Concession Card from any Transit Link office.

## Taxis

There is just shy of 30,000 taxis operating in Singapore, operated by six separate taxi companies and are a convenient transport option. Whilst they are not as cheap as public transport they are certainly a lot cheaper than buying a car! If you are accustomed to being ripped off by disreputable taxi drivers, then be reassured that all taxis are metred, with fares and tariffs being set and advertised inside the cab. Taxi drivers are all Singaporean citizens and most (but not all!) are men.

You can book a taxi using a number of ways—calling the taxi company, via SMS, its website or using an app. Once a booking is confirmed you'll be given the taxi's licence plate number as a reference. Taxis can be also flagged down on the street or you can wait in queue at a taxi stand.

The taxi fare will always include a flag-down fee plus you will be charged by distance, and also by the minute if the taxi has to stop at red lights. You will incur additional fees called surchages for the following conditions: if you book a taxi using any method, if you are travelling between midnight and 6 am, if it's a public holiday or if it's peak hours. Full details about taxi fares and charges can be viewed on the inside of taxi windows and also on the following website (www.taxisingapore.com/taxi-fare).

## Alternative car-booking services

A recent entry into the transport market is private car hire companies. These are similar to taxis, but are private vehicles that do not look like taxis. Both Uber (www.uber.com) and GrabCar (www.grab.com/sg) offer this service via their websites and mobile apps. Their fares will be listed on the booking site but make sure you check for additional fare loadings during busy times.

## Bike Sharing Schemes

Bike sharing is a new phenomenon to Singapore which has become very popular. Three companies currently operate: oBike (www.o.bike), Mobike (mobike.com/sg), and ofo (www.ofo.so). All three companies require users to download a mobile app, register as a user, pay a deposit and load credit using a credit card. It's then very easy (and cheap!) to use the app to unlock a bike using Bluetooth and be on your way! Bikes can be found throughout the country and don't need to be returned to the same spot you hired it, but it should be left in a safe location, preferably bicycle docks!

## Cars

If you're considering buying a car in Singapore, think of the price of the most expensive mass-produced car in your home country, then triple that price and add on a bit because that's approximately how much buying a car in Singapore will cost you! The reason why cars are so expensive has an easy answer—the government does not want people to own cars to avoid the traffic congestion experienced in most other cities.

The cost of buying a car is actually similar to what you pay elsewhere in the world, it's buying the Certificate of Entitlement (COE) that makes cars so expensive, and without a COE you can't drive the car. The number of COEs

available each year is controlled by the Land Transport Authority, using a bidding system. Only a set number of COEs are available so the price is determined by demand and fluctuates each quarter, but as a guide a COE for a car with a 1.6 litre engine capacity will be about $70,000. A COE lasts for ten years, which explains why it's very rare to see cars older than ten years in Singapore—if you have to pay for a new COE then you may as well buy a new car as well! On top of the cost price of the car and the COE you will also have to pay road tax, insurance and, of course, maintenance and repairs.

There is, of course, always the option of leasing a car during your stay. This is a good option for those who don't want to or can't afford to pay or borrow a lump sum upfront and has the added benefit of all maintenance and insurance being covered under the terms of the lease.

## Converting Your License

If you hold a foreign driving license then you have twelve months after arriving in Singapore to sit the Basic Theory Test (BTT) to convert it to a Singaporean license. There are three testing centres and as the slots are booked up quickly you will need to book well in advance of your preferred date and time. You will need to take with you your passport, your IC, your foreign driver's license and have a photocopy of each, along with a passport photo and either credit or debit to pay the license fee (no cash is accepted).

## Driving

How you find driving in Singapore will be very much coloured by the driving conditions in your home country. If you've come from a place that has a lot of traffic congestion and road rage then Singapore will feel like you're driving in paradise. If you've come from a rural community with little traffic then driving in Singapore will be stressful. If you've spent your whole life driving on the right-hand side of the road then you'll need to reverse everything you've learnt as Singapore drives on the left. This will also mean that you'll continually get in the wrong side of the car!

What most expat drivers will agree upon is that there are some unique quirks to driving in Singapore. Using your indicators seems to be an option rather than a necessity. When you know you're parking or stopping somewhere illegal you can just put your hazard lights on and it magically becomes legal! If you're undecided which lane to drive in just straddle the dividing line like you're PacMan eating up the dots! All joking aside, it will take some time to get used to driving in Singapore and whilst you may find yourself irritated beyond all measure with the other drivers on the road it's reassuring to know that you are in a country where true road rage is rare, so it is highly unlikely you will be verbally or physically abused over road incidents.

## Parking and Road Tolls

As another measure of reducing road congestion on the main roads throughout Singapore, tolls are charged during peak hours under the Electronic Road Pricing (ERP) scheme. The cost of the tolls change depending on the time of day and type of vehicle you are driving. Every car comes fitted with an In-Vehicle Unit (IU) into which you insert a stored value card, and the road tolls are automatically deducted each time you drive under an ERP gantry. You can find a list of the current ERP charges on the LTA website.

Unlike many countries which will have signs that tell you when you can or can't park or stop, Singapore have lines painted on the road. Make sure you get a copy of the Basic Theory book so that you can work out the difference between the zig-zag lines and the straight, yellow lines!

Parking in Singapore is rarely free and there are two methods of paying for parking. The first method uses your IU device and deducts parking charges electronically when you exit a parking station. For street parking there is a coupon system. Coupons can be purchased at service stations and convenience stores in varying amounts. You punch out the day, month, year and time and display the coupons on your dashboard. Some parking spaces are 60 cents per 30 minutes, whilst others in the busy areas may be $1.20. This means that if you park in a 60 cent area and want to pay for two hours of parking you will need to punch and display four separate coupons, all with the different half-hour times. It's very important to fully remove the punched out bits as just folding them back is an offence, as the coupon could potentially be reused.

You can top-up the stored value cards at machines in most parking garages and they can also be topped-up (for a small fee) at convenience stores. Be aware that the stored value cards have an expiry date so if the IU starts making an unusual beeping noise then check the expiry date on the back of the card.

## HOUSEHOLD HELP

Employing household help can be on either a part-time or a full-time (live-in) basis and the lure of having all your domestic duties done relatively cheaply is appealing to many expats. However, before you launch into employing a live-in Foreign Domestic Worker (FDW) you should carefully consider the pros and cons, as it is often not the idyllic arrangement that many imagine. Whilst the idea of never having to scrub the shower or mop the floor is appealing you should also consider the loss of privacy and the increased responsibility that you automatically assume when you employ a FDW.

Employing a live-in FDW is often touted as being an affordable luxury, with salaries ranging from $400 to $1,000 per month depending upon the FDW's experience. However, the cost doesn't end there as there is also a monthly levy of $265 payable to the Singaporean government. What many new employers of FDWs forget to factor in are all of the hidden costs, like providing her furniture, bedding, food and toiletries, as well as the increased costs of electricity and water as there will be an extra person living in the house.

The employer is also responsible for the costs of the FDW's home leave and her health requirements. As the employer you will be responsible for the cost of her twice yearly medical check-ups and also the cost of any medical care she may need. You must purchase mandatory health insurance coverage and the law stipulates that you will also be responsible for costs above the policy's limits of $15,000. The Ministry of Manpower website states that this limit covers 95 per cent of FDW medical claims, but you may wish to buy an additional policy which will give you more cover.

There is also a $5,000 bond but this is usually covered under your mandatory insurance policy. Averaged out over a year employing an FDW will probably cost at least $1,200 per month, provided she has no medical issues that are above your insurance limit.

If you decide that you'd like to employ a live-in FDW then you will first need to

Foreign Domestic Worker (FDW) is the official title but FDWs are commonly referred to in Singapore as 'helpers' or 'maids'.

complete the Employer's Orientation Programme (EOP), which is either a three-hour classroom session or an online tutorial. You can find details on both options at www.mom. gov.sg/services-forms/passes/work-permit-fdw/Pages/eop. aspx. Once you are ready to hire an FDW you can either use an agency or find a transfer maid through a referral. An agency will usually ask your requirements and then arrange for you to interview selected FDWs, this will usually take place on a Sunday when most FDWs have the day off. Before the interview think very carefully about what tasks are most important to you and your family and tailor your interview questions accordingly. All agencies will have different fees and conditions so always check these before deciding upon an agency.

If the idea of having a live-in helper does not appeal then there is always the option of using part-time help once or several times a week. It is illegal for FDWs to work outside the home listed on their work permit so you will need to employ a Singaporean or a permanent resident for part-time work. Many agencies offer this service, including Domestic 1 (www. domestic1.com.sg), A-Team Amahs and Cleaners (www.a-team.com.sg), Mrs Sparkles (www.mrs-sparkles.com.sg) and HomeBreeze Housekeeping (www.homebreeze.com.sg).

## HEALTH

Singapore has a world-class health system, with many people around Asia (and from further field) flying to Singapore for medical treatment. In 2014, Bloomberg ranked Singapore's health system as being the most efficient in the developed world and it's consistently ranked near the top of the rankings by the World Health Organisation (WHO).

As an expat/foreigner you are not eligible to receive subsidised health care but you can still utilise the public health system. If you need to see a general practitioner (GP) you can choose to attend a polyclinic or a private clinic, which both operate on a 'walk-in' basis. There are also many international clinics that use an appointment system and are usually staffed by expat doctors. The current fees for a polyclinic consultation for a foreigner is $41.70, and expect to pay slightly more at a private clinic. A visit to an international clinic will be more expensive than either a polyclinic or a private clinic. If you have company-issued health insurance, then check with your provider which type of clinic you should attend. Some health insurance providers have direct billing agreements with specific clinics, while other providers allow you to use any clinic but you will need to claim back the charges.

A point of difference that many expats will notice is that medicines are dispensed by the clinic, so a separate visit to the pharmacy is usually not required. You may also be surprised at the amount of medication dispensed, so feel free to refuse those which you feel are unnecessary.

Singapore has eight public hospitals—six general hospitals, one women and children's hospital, and a psychiatric hospital. In addition, there are 10 private hospitals in Singapore. If you require hospital treatment, then the choice of hospital is

> On a brief stopover in Singapore, when we were making the decision to relocate here, I had the misfortune to be taken ill and I was pleasantly surprised by the level of care I received at the Accident and Emergency (A&E) department of Mount Elizabeth hospital. Although falling ill was not a pleasant experience, we gained confidence in the Singaporean health system, and that hasn't changed during our years here.

usually at the discretion of your health insurance provider. All public and private hospitals have an A&E department, and if you have a medical emergency ,call 995 for an emergency ambulance or a hospital for private ambulance. Either way, ambulance staff will usually only stabilise the patient enough to transport them to hospital.

Singapore has lots of specialist doctors working in both the private and public sectors. The majority of doctors have been educated and/or worked overseas and are continually updating their skills and knowledge so you can have full confidence in their abilities.

Whether you require a referral from a GP for a consultation with a specialist is usually determined by your private health insurance provider, so always check with them before arranging appointments.

## Pharmacies

As most medication is dispensed at the doctor's clinic, Singaporean pharmacies in shopping centres carry much less medication than you may be accustomed to, and what they do stock will be behind the counter and require a prescription. Drugs which are sold over-the-counter in many countries, such as ibuprofen, may require a prescription.

### Staying Healthy

The best health tip anyone can have when moving to Singapore is to drink water and plenty of it. The temperature and the humidity are incredibly dehydrating so always carry a bottle of water with you.

The second best health tip is to use insect repellent to avoid contracting dengue fever. Singapore does its absolute best to keep the number of mosquitoes low with weekly fogging (insecticide spraying) but there are still regular outbreaks of dengue.

And, thirdly, be sun-safe. Wear sunscreen and stay out of the sun between 11 am and 2 pm.

## MONEY, MONEY, MONEY

The Singaporean currency is the dollar, with one hundred cents making up every dollar. Coins are issued in 5, 10, 20, 50 cents as well as $1. Notes are issued in $2, $5, $10, $50, $100, $1,000 and $10,000 denominations, although I've yet to see either of the highest two bank notes personally!

Singapore has a 7 per cent Goods and Services Tax (GST) which is included in the purchase price of goods. The exception to this is in restaurants which will sometimes have ++ next to the price, and this indicates that you will need to add on 7 per cent for GST as well as a 10 per cent service charge. As there is a service charge added to the bill, you do not need to tip in Singapore.

### Bank Accounts

At the top of the expat's to-do list is usually 'Open a local bank account' and it's probably something you will do during your first days in Singapore. The three largest banks in Singapore are DBS/POSB, UOB and OCBC but there are many others to choose from including ANZ, Standard Chartered and Citibank. Before you choose a bank, visit their websites and consider the following factors:

- Nearby branches
- ATM network. You will only be able to use ATMs that belong to your bank so choosing a bank with an extensive network will make your life easier.
- Fees, charges and minimum balances.

Once you've decided which bank you prefer give them a call and check what documentation you will need to take with you to open an account. To open a new account you will need to visit a branch, taking with you the documents the bank requires which at a minimum will be your passport and your employment pass. It is usually a requirement that the account be in the name of employment pass holder, although a spouse can be a joint account holder. It's best to visit a branch earlier in the day as queues can be lengthy, although some will assign you a queue number and send you an SMS when it's your turn. The good thing is that once your account is open and you've activated your internet banking options you may never have to visit a branch again!

## Tax

The tax system in Singapore is regulated by the Internal Revenue Authority of Singapore (IRAS) and, happily, the tax rates here are less than many other countries.

The amount of tax you pay is dependent upon whether you are a resident or a non-resident for tax purposes. You are considered to be a resident if you are either Singaporean, a permanent resident, or a foreigner who was in Singapore for more than 183 days of the previous tax year. If you don't meet any of these criteria then you will be taxed as a non-resident. As a tax resident any foreign income earned that is brought into Singapore is taxable.

Singapore uses progressive tax rates, so the more you earn the more you pay. The percentages paid is set to rise in 2017 but in broad terms the tax rate ranges from zero to 22 per cent of annual earnings. For exact information and up-to-date tax rates visit the IRAS website (www.iras.gov.sg)

which has detailed and easily understandable information specific to foreigners.

## Lodging Your Tax Return

The Singapore tax year is the same as the calendar year, so it runs from January 1 until December 31 with tax returns due for filing by April 15 each year. By March 1 your employer will provide you with a copy of your IR8A form, which details your earnings for the previous tax year. If you are required to file a tax return the IRAS will advise you by March 31 in writing, by phone or via SMS. You can then complete the form either on paper or via the online portal. Once the IRAS has processed your tax return they will issue a Notice of Assessment (NOA) which will detail how much tax you owe and when and how to pay it.

### Support Networks

Connecting with people and finding new friends is one way of helping to alleviate the culture shock which may descend once the flurry of reorganising your life is finished. Fortunately, expat communities are used to welcoming newcomers, and other expats are the best source of advice you will find. If possible try and form some connections before you move to Singapore, and this is where social media is extremely beneficial. There are numerous different websites, forums and groups that have been set up by Singapore expats for other Singapore expats that provide advice and opinions, as well as some that organise social activities and get-togethers. Admittedly, not every page will suit everyone so keep looking until you find one that suits you.

There are also 'real world' support groups if you prefer your interaction to be face-to-face! Some companies have an informal policy of existing staff reaching out to new arrivals and making them welcome. If you have children who are at school then check what groups are available within the school community as most will have lots of parent activities such as newcomer coffee mornings, book clubs, and the like. Another place to find a network is through the various associations, such as ANZA (Australian and New Zealand Association) and the AWA (American Women's Association), which arrange coffee mornings, sporting groups, book clubs, heritage tours, craft clubs, photography clubs, etc... No matter what your interests are you will be sure to find an existing group to join!

# FOOD

❝Nobody in Singapore drinks Singapore Slings. It's one of the first things you find out there. What you do in Singapore is eat. It's a really food-crazy culture, where all of this great food is available in a kind of hawker-stand environment..❞

**— Anthony Bourdain**

Singaporeans adore food. Sure, everyone everywhere adores food but Singaporeans take it to a whole new level. I think it would be fair to say that Singaporean life revolves around food far more than other cultures. And if they aren't actually eating at the time then they may well be talking about food! It's quite common to be asked whether you have 'taken your breakfast/lunch yet?' by a local. Whilst this may seem odd to those of us new to the island it's the equivalent of asking "how are you today?" and demonstrates just how important food is to Singaporeans.

There's one main reason why the local population is so focussed on food—because the food here is good! The food in Singapore is so good that even Singapore-hating William Gibson (who wrote the article 'Disneyland with the Death Penalty' in Wired magazine) had to praise it. Despite writing off the rest of Singapore as "boring" he said that the food was "something to write home about".

Singaporean food is multi-cultural. It reflects the influences of all the different cultures that have ever lived on the island, not just the Chinese, Malay and Indian people. Some local dishes, like *roti prata* which is of Indian heritage, are a direct influence of one particular culture but most dishes are a fusion of different cultures. Over time, recipes have been adapted

to suit Singaporeans' tastes and also in response to the availability of ingredients. For example, some Chinese dishes which traditionally would never have included chilli peppers are now served spicy to suit the local palate.

## EATING LIKE A LOCAL

It should come as no surprise to anyone that the staple foods of Singapore are rice and noodles. Almost every meal a local person eats will have one or the other in it. Rice is probably just ahead as the preferred staple, but noodles come a very close second.

Steamed white rice is the most common side dish. You'll find it served alongside all manner of dishes, including both meat and vegetable options. A staple stall in any hawker centre or food court is the economy (or mixed rice) stall, which serves steamed white rice with your choice of accompanying dishes. Sometimes rice is fried, as in fried rice. Sometimes it's soaked in coconut milk (*nasi lemak*). And sometimes it's mixed with chicken stock and some lard as it is with chicken rice. Any which way you try it, it will be delicious!

The noodles popularly used in Singapore cooking fall into two broad categories—egg noodles or rice noodles. If you've come from a country where 'Singapore noodles' features on the menu of Asian restaurants then you're in for a shock as no such dish exists in Singapore! Some of the popular types of noodles you'll find are:

- **Bee Hoon:** made from rice flour the noodles are long, thin and white. Often used in fish soups.
- **Chor Bee Hoon:** Thicker than regular *bee hoon*. Made from rice flour.
- **Kway Teow:** Flat, wide and white rice noodle, like white fettucine. It's often also called *hor fun*.
- **Mee:** fresh egg noodle which is thick, yellow and long. A noodle that suits a variety of dishes from soups to dry dishes. The noodle of choice for *Hokkien mee*.
- **Mee Tai Bak:** A white noodle that is short and thick and mostly used in laksa.
- **Mee Pok:** a thin flat yellow egg noodle a bit like fettucine.
- **Mee Kia:** a thin, long noodle that is commonly used in fried dishes.

At the end of the day, unless you're trying to recreate a local dish at home (or have gluten or egg allergies), you don't need to be too concerned about knowing all the different

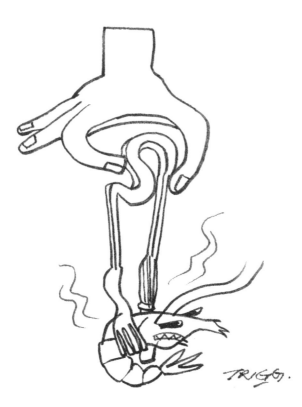

## Chopsticks, Forks or Fingers?

For those people who are accustomed to eating with knives and forks then you will be relieved to learn that you won't be forced to eat with chopsticks. Every hawker centre and food court I've visited supplies both. Do give chopsticks a try, though, as it's not as tricky as it looks and as you will probably eat slower it makes you savour the yummy food! When putting your chopsticks down you should try to avoid having them crossed as some people consider it bad manners. Lay them on your plate next to each other. Also—and this is very important—never stand your chopsticks upright in a bowl of rice. This is how a bowl of rice is served to the spirit of a deceased person and will cause great offence.

It's also OK to use the fingers of your right hand to eat your meal (but never your left hand!), especially for Indian cuisine. This is a technique I've yet to master but the idea is that you gather a bit of curry with some rice and shape it into a ball using the tips of your fingers and your thumb, which is then popped in your mouth. Serving spoons are still used to transfer each portion from the communal plate, though!

noodle varieties. Just order what looks or sounds good to you and enjoy! (If you do want to get to grips with the different noodles, then check out the noodle section in the fridge at your local supermarket.)

Chicken and seafood are the two most common sources of protein used in local food. This is because they are acceptable to all faiths (but obviously not for vegetarians!). As Hindus don't eat beef and Muslims don't eat pork, chicken and seafood appeal to the bulk of the population. However, most types of meat are available in any hawker centre or food court, so keep searching until you find what you want. The good news is that you won't usually encounter too many unusual animals or animal parts. Tarantulas, red ants, snake, and monkey may be available in other Asian countries but not in Singapore. If you really want to lash out on some exotic meats you could look for frog's legs or pig organ soup.

## Vegetarian Food

If you are a vegetarian you will be pleased to know that a lot of Singaporean food are suitable for vegetarians. Tofu and 'mock' meats made from bean curd are widely available in hawker centres and food courts. The mixed or economy rice stall is a good place to start if you're nervous about what to try as you can pick out which dishes you want. As many Hindus choose to not eat any meat the Indian stall is also a good option for vegetarians.

## Classic Singapore Dishes

**Chicken rice** is exactly what the name says it is: chicken and rice. But don't mistake this for a boring dish: the secret is in the delicious flavoured rice, usually cooked in chicken stock and chicken fat. You can order either Hainanese chicken (sometimes called 'white chicken') which is poached chicken, or soy roasted chicken with a darker and crispy skin.

**Singapore chilli crab** is famous around the world. You will usually get to pick out your own still-alive crab (or have the staff do it for you) which will be cooked in a spicy sauce made from chillies, tomato sauce, lime juice and egg. Eat it with your hands and buy some steamed/fried buns (called *mantou*) to mop up the sauce.

**Fish head curry** is exactly what it sounds like: a whole fish head (and a decent portion of its body) cooked in a spicy and aromatic curry that usually includes a few vegetables. For those coming from Western countries where eating of animals is limited to just the flesh this can be a disconcerting experience. However, you aren't obliged to eat the brain,

eyeballs and tongue as there's plenty of meat on the fish. It's fortunate that my husband and I stopped at two children as the cheeks are their favourite part of this dish!

**Kaya toast** is a favourite breakfast food. *Kaya* is a jam made from coconut milk, eggs, pandan leaf and sugar. *Kaya* toast is often served with a couple of soft boiled eggs and *kopi* (coffee).

**Popiah** is similar to a spring roll and is prepared to order so that you are able to customise it. A paper-thin wheat flour wrapper is filled with thin strips of cooked *bangkwang* (sweet Chinese turnip), as well as tofu, pork, shrimp, beans sprouts and omelette. It's topped with a lettuce leaf and a sweet sauce.

**Carrot cake** doesn't contain a single carrot and it's not even a cake! It's called 'cake' as it is made from grated white radish (known in Chinese as white carrot) mixed with rice flour which sets to form a solid 'cake'. This is then broken up and stir-fried with egg, soy sauce, pepper and chilli sauce. It looks a little like a broken up omelette. White carrot cake has a sprinkling of soy sauce, while dark carrot cake has lots of thick and sweet soy sauce.

**Satay** is thinly sliced meat (beef, chicken or mutton usually) on a stick cooked over an open flame. They are served with a delicious peanut sauce, cucumber and red onion and are one of my family's favourite hawker foods!

**Char kway teow** is kway teow noodles stir-fried (hence the '*char*', which means 'fried' in Hokkien) and can come with seafood, chicken and/or beef.

**Hor fun** refers to *hor fun* noodles cooked in soy sauce and served in a soupy gravy. The dish is usually served with seafood and leafy green vegetables but can also be made with beef, chicken or pork. Seafood *hor fun* is a favourite hawker dish for my daughters, and they have never managed to finish an entire serving in four years!

**Bak kut teh** is pork ribs served in a delicious soup that is a breakfast favourite, but can be eaten at any meal. Hokkein *bak kut teh* has a dark soup, while the Teochew version is clear and a little spicy as it has pepper added.

**Oyster omelette** is what its name suggests: an omelette with oysters.

**Hokkien mee** combines both egg and rice noodles stir-fried with shrimp, bean shoots, fish cake, and pork fat. This is probably the dish that has inspired the Western dish called 'Singapore noodles'.

**Nasi biryani** is of Indian origin and this dish has delicious aromatic long-grain rice that is usually served with chicken or mutton curry.

**Roti prata** is another dish that is Indian in origin but has become a Singaporean favourite. *Roti prata* is an unleavened flat bread that is cooked until crispy. Traditionally it's served with a curry sauce. Many stallholders offer roti prata with

*Roti prata* is a Singapore favourite. The crispy flat bread is dunked in the accompanying curry sauce.

a variety of fillings such as cheese, egg, bananas and mushrooms.

*Rojak* (means 'mixture' in Malay) comes in two varieties: Indian and Chinese. Both are essentially fried salads. The Chinese version combines pieces of pineapple, cucumber, red and green chillies with a sauce made from tamarind, dried shrimp paste, sugar, salt and lemon juice, topped with chopped peanuts. When ordering Indian rojak the customer selects a mixture of ingredients (usually vegetables, seafood and tofu choices) which are then quickly stir-fried so that everything is hot and crispy. It's served with a sweet chilli dip on the side.

## Local Desserts

The **durian** is the king of fruits, known globally for its pungent smell. So 'unique' is the smell that the durian is banned from being carried on public transport in Singapore. I can't quite put into words precisely what it smells like, but should you be anywhere in Singapore (usually a hawker centre or wet market) and think to yourself 'what is that smell?' then you're probably in close proximity to a durian. However, despite its aroma offending my Western sinuses, most Singaporeans adore durian. A durian is a large fruit with a thick, spiky husk. Inside are several pieces of soft, juicy flesh. Those who have tried it say that it has a creamy texture and a taste not dissimilar to custard. I'm happy to report that everyone says it tastes a lot better than it smells!

*Ice kachang* is ground-up ice flavoured with a variety of syrups and a dollop of condensed milk on top.

The durian season is typically between June and August, with a minor season between December to February. You will find them sold at durian shops or in the supermarkets during these months.

Underneath the ice are usually a few treats such as sweet corn kernels, jelly and beans.

**Snow ice** is a block of flavoured ice shaved into a bowl and topped with a sauce. Popular flavours are strawberry, chocolate, mango and durian. This is my kids' favourite hawker centre dessert.

### Drinks

Whilst ordering a local coffee seems daunting at first, especially as there are rarely signs helping you to decode a *Kopi O* from a *Kopi Po*, with a little bit of knowledge you'll be ordering like a local in no time! If Starbucks can have its own coffee vocabulary, so can Singapore!

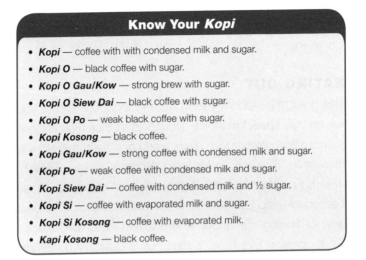

**Know Your *Kopi***

- ***Kopi*** — coffee with with condensed milk and sugar.
- ***Kopi O*** — black coffee with sugar.
- ***Kopi O Gau/Kow*** — strong brew with sugar.
- ***Kopi O Siew Dai*** — black coffee with sugar.
- ***Kopi O Po*** — weak black coffee with sugar.
- ***Kopi Kosong*** — black coffee.
- ***Kopi Gau/Kow*** — strong coffee with condensed milk and sugar.
- ***Kopi Po*** — weak coffee with condensed milk and sugar.
- ***Kopi Siew Dai*** — coffee with condensed milk and ½ sugar.
- ***Kopi Si*** — coffee with evaporated milk and sugar.
- ***Kopi Si Kosong*** — coffee with evaporated milk.
- ***Kapi Kosong*** — black coffee.

For tea drinkers, just replace '*kopi*' with '*teh*'. If it all seems too much to decipher just tell the stallholder what you want, for example '*kopi* with milk and two sugars, please'.

***Teh Tarik*** means 'pulled tea' in Malay. The tea mixed with either evaporated or condensed milk is poured from a great height in an up-and-down motion, which causes bubbles on the surface

**Lime juice** is an excellent refreshing accompaniment to oily dishes as the citric acid helps to wash away the film. The juice of fresh limes is usually sweetened with either syrup or sugar to make the drink less tart. Lime juice is definitely my favourite Singaporean drink!

**Sugarcane juice** is a traditional Asian drink with a long history and usually found in hawker centres. Fresh sugarcane sticks are put through a press that extracts all of the juice. It's a sweet, refreshing juice that is sometimes served with some lime on the side.

**Tiger beer** is the national beer of Singapore and available everywhere! If you aren't a fan of Tiger, then most drink stalls will also carry the common brands like Heineken and Carlsberg.

## EATING OUT

The great thing about eating out in Singapore is that you will be truly spoilt for choice. Due to its multicultural society, you can find pretty much every world cuisine here—Nonya, Japanese, Spanish, Indonesian, Korean, Indian, Turkish, Italian, French, Mexican, British fish and chips, American barbeque—you just have to know where to look. The best way of finding out about where to eat is to ask people. Singaporeans love food. Eating out is basically a national sport, with everybody having their favourite food stalls and restaurants. Singaporeans also love to talk about food. Ask any taxi uncle where to eat and they are usually more than happy to tell you the best, and cheapest, places to eat.

Eating out can be super cheap ($3 for a bowl of noodles) or super expensive (think three figures). There's also a vast range of good food in between those two price points. As a guide, always expect to pay more the closer you are to the tourist areas, so if you are after a bargain meal then heading away from Orchard or Marina Bay will save you money.

"The biggest empty space, the biggest gap in what should be a premier and always vibrant food scene in America is that we don't have hawker centres like they do in Singapore, basically food courts where mom and pop specialists can set up shop in fairly hygienic little stalls all up to health code making one dish they've been doing forever and ever."
—Anthony Bourdain

### Hawker Centres

Singapore is famous for its hawker centres, with most visitors eating in at least one during their stay. The hawker centre has its origins in the mobile food carts that could be

pushed around different locations. The hawker would let people know he was around by ringing a bell, banging a stick or just yelling out. 'Hawker' means someone who sells something. As Singapore moved toward becoming a First World nation, stallholders were moved into permanent centres and these became known as 'hawker centres'. By centralising the vendors in a permanent setting a close eye could be kept on the food hygiene standards. People could still buy traditional Singaporean street food but it was less likely to come with a side serve of food poisoning!

Hawker centres (also known as food centres) are located all around Singapore and provide a great way to mix with the locals. Most hawker centres are sheltered, although Newton Food Centre has an open area in the centre. They can get hot, noisy and smoky, but it's all part and parcel of the hawker centre experience. If you are bothered by the heat then keep an eye out for a table near a fan. There's no dress code so

To 'chope' is to reserve seats or a table. The favourite method of reserving seats is to place either a packet of tissues or an umbrella on the table. Do not presume that someone has merely left their tissues behind and take a seat as this is the height of rudeness in Singapore! Respect the 'chope'!

feel free to dress comfortably!

For the uninitiated, a visit to a hawker centre can be a little overwhelming, so if possible have a friend join you so they can show you how the system works. You can order from any stall in a hawker market, although some centres have touts who seat you and present you with a menu as if you were in a restaurant. Touting is illegal but it does still happen in the big touristy centres. You are not under any obligation to order from the person that shows you to an empty table and gives you a menu. Each stall usually specialises in a few dishes, so feel free to order from a couple of different stalls.

The best way to start is to simply walk around looking at all the stalls and what they sell. Each stall will have photos of what they sell, and you can always ask the stall-holder for

## Grades and Labels

Each food outlet in Singapore is assessed annually and receives a hygiene rating from the National Environment Agency (NEA). An A is for outlets that receive 85% or better, B for 70–80%, C for 50–69% and D for less than 50%. Whilst this is the government's rating system, the locals have their own tongue-in-cheek system—A is for avoid, B is for bad, C is for 'can', and D is for delicious. Some locals swear that any stall who has the time to achieve an A grade mustn't have much business as they have too much time to clean! Food outlets are required to display their grade at the front of the stall. This will let customers know in advance what the hygiene standards of the outlet are so that they can make an informed decision.

The other main sign that you will routinely see at food outlets is one indicating that it is halal. The certification is awarded by MUIS (Islamic Religious Council of Singapore). If you are of the Islamic faith, look for the halal symbol. If you are not Islamic you are welcome to eat from halal-certified stalls, but please be mindful not to mix the plates and utensils from the halal stall with those from non-halal stalls.

more information if you're unsure what is in the dish. When you see something that you'd like to eat, order it from the stall-holder and give them your table number (which you will find on the top of the table). Unless the stall has a sign saying 'self-service', the stall-holder will normally bring your meal to your table. Payment is usually when they bring the food, but some stall-holders may ask for payment up front.

Drinks are sold at separate stalls and drink stalls usually sell beer, soft drinks, juices and sometimes premixed spirits in a bottle. It's also acceptable to bring your own alcohol with you. I've seen many people open a bottle of wine or duty-free scotch at hawker centres!

Feel free to customise the dish to your taste. You can ask the stall-holder to add more or less chilli or to serve the chilli on the side. Most stall-holders are more than happy to do this for you—just ask!

Every area in Singapore will have a hawker centre but it's also worth visiting some of the larger ones, even if they

Food courts are usually located in shopping malls, like this one in Wisma Atria. They are usually self-service, so customers wait at the stall while their food is being prepared before carrying the food back to their choped table.

charge a bit more. If you aren't sure which stall or dish to eat then joining the longest queue will undoubtedly lead you to the best food! Some hawker centres to try:

- **Newton Food Centre** (500 Clemenceau Ave North, 229495) is one of the most famous hawker centres and has a variety of stalls with an emphasis on seafood. Most stalls open from midday through to midnight.
- **Maxwell Road Food Centre** (1 Kadayanallur St, 069184) is near Chinatown. Open from 8 am to 10 pm.
- **Satay by the Bay** is a new hawker centre in the grounds of Gardens By The Bay. The drink stall is open 24 hours a day while the food stalls are open from 11 am to 10 pm. There is a huge variety of food stalls but the highlight is the satay stall!
- **Lau Pa Sat** (18 Raffles Quay, 048582) is also known as Telok Ayer Market and is housed in a 19th-century octagonal-shaped building. There is a huge variety of food stalls, and in the evening Boon Tat Street is closed to traffic and transforms into 'Satay Street'. The market is open 24 hours (but not all food stalls trade around the clock).
- **Chinatown Food Street** is an undercover dining area in Smith Street. Open from 11 am until 11 pm, the street has a selection of stalls and shops serving a wide variety of local dishes.
- **Tiong Bahru Food Centre** (30 Seng Poh Road, 168898; www.tiongbahru.market) is located above

Tiong Bahru Market and is renowned for its authentic and delicious local fare. Many stalls have long queues of locals, which is always a good sign! Open from 8 am to 8 pm.

- **East Coast Lagoon Food Village** (1220 East Coast Parkway, 468960) is an ideal place to take a break from a cycling trip. Open from 11 am to 11 pm daily.

## Food Courts

A food court is an indoor, air-conditioned hawker centre. The main difference between the two is that food courts are usually self-service, so when you order from the counter you wait for your meal to be prepared. Just like in hawker centres, drinks will be sold at a separate stall, or in fancy food courts someone on a Segway may come around selling them!

In both food courts and hawker centres there are a few types of stalls that you'll usually find. There will always be a drinks stall. The economy or mixed rice stall has a wide range of meat and vegetable dishes which are served alongside white rice. You usually have the option of one meat dish and two or three vegetable dishes for a set price. The dishes usually don't have labels so you may need to ask what each dish is if you are unsure. The chicken rice stall will sell chicken rice, and sometimes offer roasted duck as well.

## Coffee Shops

Singaporean coffee shops may not exactly match the image that you have in your mind as they don't sell lattes or cakes! Coffee shops (or *kopitiam*) are like a small

When eating at both hawker centres and food courts bring your own wet wipes or tissues, as napkins are not typically supplied. If you forget yours then there will often be someone selling them, which is one way that the disabled in Singapore earn a living.

hawker centre, and are usually integrated within HDB estates. The coffee shop is one of the popular gathering spots for locals and if the football (or soccer) is on you'll usually find a crowd gathered there to watch the match. Whilst not the same as a British pub, the vibe is essentially what British people call their 'local'.

A coffee shop will have a few different food stalls but there are three main types of stalls that you will almost always find. The first (and usually the cheapest option) is the economy or mixed rice stall that you'll also find in hawker centres. Steamed rice served with a meat dish and two or three vegetables of your choice for a set price. The *tze char* stall sells a variety of Chinese dishes cooked to order and is usually a little more expensive than the economy rice stall. Popular menu items include steamboat and seafood-based dishes and as the portions are often quite large *tze char* is a good option to share with friends. The third major food stall is the Indian/Muslim stall which will serves a variety of dishes from Indian or Muslim origin such as *roti prata* and the *briyani*. Some coffee shops will also have a Western-style stall that sells steaks, chops and various Western dishes and in recent times both Japanese and pizza stalls have also popped up.

The balance of stalls in any particular coffee shop is usually determined by its customer base, for example the more Chinese people who eat there the more Chinese options you will find.

As well as the food stalls there will always be a drink stall. They will usually sell a variety of beer, soft drink, coffee and juices. You can order either at the drink stall or look for the person with a change bag around their waist and place your order with him/her. Occasionally you'll find 'beer ladies' who are representatives of beer companies and are easily identifiable as they will be wearing the beer company's logo on their clothes.

## Trays—to return or not to return?

Once, in the early days of my time in Singapore, after I had finished my meal at McDonald's, I cleared the table of debris, placed it on the tray and emptied it all into the bin. The lovely aunty whose job it is to clear the tables took me aside and explained that this was her job and if I kept clearing the tables she would be out of a job.

All hawker stalls (and most restaurants) will be happy to package your food to take away. If you want your food to go you should say either 'da bao, please!' or 'tapau, please! If you are eating at a restaurant or hawker centre and can't finish your meal, you can always ask for a doggy bag. Whilst this may not be acceptable in many countries it's common practice in Singapore.

Having someone else clear your table of rubbish and trays is pretty much how it has been in Singapore up until very recently. In 2013 the National Environment Agency (NEA) introduced the 'Tray Return Initiative' which encourages patrons of hawker centres to return their trays to a central point in the centre. The initiative did not meet with universal acceptance. Many felt that it would leave the cleaners out of a job and others felt that food prices should be lower if they had to clean up after themselves.

Regardless of the objections the NEA is committed to providing a central tray return area in each hawker centre with the aim of encouraging 'social graciousness'. If the cleaner doesn't whip it all off your table for you (which happens often) then clear the table yourself and place the tray in the tray return area.

## Restaurants

There is no shortage of restaurants in Singapore. Name a cuisine and you'll more than likely find a restaurant here making it. It may not be 100 per cent authentic but it should sate your yearning for food from home! As with many things the best way to find out where the best restaurants are is to ask people. Restaurants come and go quickly here and I've been caught out more than once when I've headed to a favourite restaurant only to find it closed or a new restaurant in its place!

Just like with housing and shopping, the closer you are to the tourist areas, the more you will pay for a meal. If you decide to eat at either Boat or Clarke Quay then you will definitely pay more than if you choose a restaurant in the heartlands. The bad news with restaurants is that your bill will more than likely be larger than you are used to. On the bright side, you won't need to leave a tip as a service charge will usually be already incorporated.

In recent years there has been an influx of 'celebrity chef' restaurants, particularly in the Marina Bays Shoppes and Harbourfont malls. Jamie Oliver, Wolfgang Puck, Luke Mangan, Gordon Ramsay, Joel Robuchon, and Tetsuya Wakudo are just a few of the big names who have opened restaurants here. So, if you are a fan of dining in a restaurant owned by a celebrity chef then you will be spoiled for choice!

When writing this chapter I asked on social media for suggestions of 'eat streets' or streets with a choice of restaurants. To say I was inundated is an understatement! It's safe to say that no matter where in Singapore you are there will be an area of restaurants not too far away. Whilst it would be impossible to list all of them here I've included a few suggestions to set you on your way:

- Bussorah Street and Haji Lane in Kampong Glam
- Greenwood Avenue
- Dempsey Hill
- Holland Village has two streets of restaurants—Jalan Merah Saga (sometimes called Chip Bee Gardens) and Lorong Mambong.
- Duxton Hill
- Robertson Quay
- Tanjong Katong Road
- Joo Chiat Road
- Keong Saik Street
- Club Street

Another great source of knowledge on restaurants is the multitude of websites devoted to reviewing and recommending places to eat. It's rare to eat a meal anywhere in Singapore now and not spot at least one person taking a photo of their meal which will inevitably end up online somewhere. There are a plethora of food reviewer blogs out there but a couple of reputable sites are:

- www.ladyironchef.com
- www.hungrygowhere.com

## Tipping

Singapore does not have a tipping culture as the service charge is already included in the bill. It's OK to round up the bill a dollar or two, but there's no need to give a 10% tip like you would in other countries.

One thing to look out for is ++ next to the price in a menu. This indicates that the written price does NOT include either the 7% Goods and Services Tax (GST) or the 10% service charge. So if you see a ++ you need to do some mental arithmetic and add an extra 17% to know the full price of what you intend to order.

## Fast Food

Before we moved to Singapore I had been told that the local population ate at hawker centres all the time, so the proliferation of fast food outlets surprised me. In particular the number of different fried chicken stores was eye-opening—there are fried chicken franchises from at least three US states (Kentucky, Louisiana and Texas)! All of the big Western (OK, they are almost exclusively American) fast foods chains have a presence here—McDonald's, Pizza Hut, Dominoes, Burger King, Krispy Kreme, to name but a few. There are also fast food outlets from Japan (Mos Burgers), Philippines (Jollibee) and other points of the globe.

If you think fast food tastes the same wherever in the world you are then you may be (slightly) mistaken. Most fast food outlets in Singapore don't use pork products, so your pizza will more than likely come with turkey bacon instead. Some franchises also customise their menu for the local market by including items or ingredients that Singaporeans like. My kids are quite taken with the seaweed shaker that McDonald's often sell as an option with fries!

One thing that is a rarity for fast food outlets here is a drive thru. There are a few McDonald's outlets that have a drive thru but with most people not owning a car it just isn't a priority in Singapore. Don't be disheartened, though, as lots of fast food restaurants have home delivery, including McDonald's and KFC.

If you want home-delivered food beyond pizza or fast food then there are lots of good options. The online site Food Panda (foodpanda.sg) is a portal for many different restaurants' home delivery services. My only word of warning with any home delivery food is that the wait time is often quite lengthy so it is best to plan as far in advance as you can.

## Cafes and Bakeries

It's not just hawker centres, fast food or restaurants as Singapore has an ever-expanding number of cafes and bakeries. There are lots of franchise cafes that you may already be familiar with such as Starbucks but there also local ones such as Cedele's, Bakerzin, Coffee Club and Coffee Connection.

The one area of change I've seen in my four years is the rise of the independent café and bakery. Four years ago finding a small independent café was almost impossible but they seem to be popping up everywhere at the moment, often in unexpected and hidden places. All of these places, whether they are part of a chain or not, will serve a variety of hot and cold drinks, plus other bakery items.

## FOOD SHOPPING

Shopping for food has been the most difficult part of settling in to Singapore for me. It has literally brought me to tears. The main cause of my grocery shopping angst is not being able to buy all of my groceries in one place, as there is no 'one-stop shopping' in Singapore. I visit different supermarket chains and branches for different things, as well as buying some things online and visiting the wet market. Learning the art of grocery shopping is an important step to feeling at home in Singapore!

### Plastic shopping bags

Singapore does not yet have a 'bring your own bag' shopping culture, with many supermarkets using two plastic bags for heavy items. However, you can (and should!) use your own reusable shopping bags whenever possible. Some supermarkets offer a (very small) discount if you bring your own bags but at this stage the savings are not nearly enough to encourage widespread use of reusable bags. Hopefully, in the future there will be a greater emphasis on discouraging the use of plastic bags.

## Supermarkets

There are a few different supermarket chains in Singapore, and within each chain there are different brands that offer shopping experiences and products. Supermarkets are usually located on the lowest level of a shopping mall.

Dairy Farm International Holdings owns the brands Cold Storage and Marketplace. **Marketplace** is the fanciest supermarket chain and stores are located in the bigger shopping malls along Orchard Road. They stock a large range of imported items and specialty foods with a large delicatessen area and good quality meats. Some stores have a bakery concession inside. Overall it is the most expensive supermarket brand. Check for its locations at the website (https://coldstorage.com.sg/store-locations/3/market-place).

**Cold Storage** (www.coldstorage.com.sg) can be found all over Singapore, and is the predominant brand in areas where expats typically live. The size of each store varies, as do the products each store carry so you can't assume that what you can buy at one store you can get from another. They usually carry a decent range of imported and local products. Some stores cater for a particular market; as an example, the Cold Storage stores in both Ngee Ann City and Liang Court stock lots of Japanese products as they have many Japanese customers. There are also Cold Storage Express stores which are smaller stores that focus upon stocking gourmet products.

Opening hours vary between stores, with the majority opening at 9 am and closing at 10 pm. Several are open 24 hours such as Jelita, Aperia, Holland Village, Rail Mall, Serangoon NEX and Cluny Court.

**Fairprice** (www.fairprice.com.sg) is the direct competitor of Cold Storage. It's operated by the National Trade

Union Council (NTUC) and has several different styles of supermarkets throughout Singapore. Fairprice Finest has large, bright, well-stocked stores with a great range of products that include meat, fish, fruit and vegetables. Fairprice Xtra is very similar to Finest but they have an extra section which stocks electronics, homewares, and a small range of clothes. Fairprice is the base brand and the one that has the most stores. The stores are a bit smaller and crowded than either Finest or Xtra and they carry more Asian products and less Western ones, consequently their prices are usually cheaper.

Opening hours of Fairprice stores vary but the majority are open from 8 am until 11 pm. There are also a large number of stores that are open 24 hours.

**Giant** is owned by Dairy Farm International Holdings and has over sixty stores across the island and operate on a model similar to Fairprice (despite being owned by the same parent company of Cold Storage). Giant Express are small stores that stock necessities. Giant Super stores are basic supermarkets that you'll mainly find in the heartlands. Giant Hyper are large grocery stores as well as discount department stores selling everything from electronics to sporting goods to clothes and books.

All Giant stores are open between 9 am and 10.30 pm but

## Supermarket Loyalty Cards

Both Cold Storage and Fairprice have their own loyalty cards. Fairprice has the Fairprice Plus card, while Cold Storage uses PAssion Card. When we first moved it took me several weeks of daily trips to Cold Storage to understand that "do you have PAssion Card?" was referring to a loyalty card and not a proposition from the cashier. Both schemes work the same with points being earned for each dollar you spend in store. The points have a monetary value which you can use to pay for some of your shopping. It's well worth getting both of these loyalty cards.

many Giant Super and Express stores are open 24 hours.

**Sheng Siong** (www.shengsiong.com.sg) is a growing supermarket chain which has many of its stores open around the clock. Originally started by a family as a new business when their pig-farming business ended, the chain offers a 'no frills' approach to grocery shopping with fewer staff and Western goods but also rock-bottom prices. Sheng Siong is an excellent place to save money on your grocery bill.

The majority of Sheng Siong stores are open 24 hours a day, but several have shorter operating hours of 7 am until 10 pm.

**Mustafa Centre** (145 Syed Alwi Road, 207704; www.mustafa.com.sg) is a treasure trove. You never know what you will find. It's a terrific place to find herbs, spices and Indian ingredients but it also stocks lots of imported Western products. My Kiwi friends tell me you can often find New Zealand favourites there. The fruit and vegetable section is cheaper than most of the other supermarkets. Mustafa is open 24 hours daily.

## Online Shopping

One big change to grocery shopping I have noticed during my time here is the increase in online shopping. If you decide not to have a car then online grocery shopping is a brilliant option for you as it avoids the logistics of getting your shopping from the store to your home. Even if you do have a car it saves you having to leave the house! Ordering is usually straightforward, payment is via credit card and delivery is usually within a day or two. All of the supermarket chains except Mustafa now have an online retail store which sell most of the same products as their stores, including fresh produce. Another popular online grocery retailer is **Redmart** (www.redmart.com). They don't have stores but have built a reputable online business that provides good quality products and great customer service.

## Warehouse Stores

A new arrival in the Singapore grocery shopping scene is warehouse stores, which operate similar to the US store Costco. You will have to pay a joining fee, but if you have the space to store bulk quantities and the means to get them home then shopping at a warehouse store may be a good way to cut down your grocery bills. **Fairprice Warehouse Club** (1 Joo Koon Circle, 629116) stocks grocery items, electrical goods, sporting goods and alcohol. **Big Box** (1 Venture Ave, 608521) is a series of separate stores inside one building all with a 'box' theme. In addition to grocery items there are clothes, furniture, electrical goods, gift wares, and even mobility aids (humorously called 'Silver Box').

## Wet Markets

A wet market is a market that sells fresh fruit, vegetables, meat and fish. They are called 'wet' from the days when ice was used to chill the produce which would then make the floor wet as it melted. Today refrigeration is used but the wet markets are still not for the squeamish. Most markets smell. On busy days when the produce is freshest the wet markets can get very crowded, noisy and hot. It can be a very overwhelming experience at first but perseverance and developing a relationship with the stall holders is the key to being a successful wet market shopper. For a novice it's a good idea to take an experienced marketer with you as they can show you how the market works.

A wet market is the best place to buy the freshest produce at the cheapest prices, but it is an accepted part of the

culture that there are three prices in a wet market—local price, helper/maid price, and *ang moh* price. Whilst it may be irritating that as an expat you are expected to pay more than a Singaporean you'll still make big savings by shopping at a wet market, and you'll also help small businesses stay in business. I once conducted a price comparison for a basket of fresh produce and buying at a wet market was less than half the price of buying the same items at Cold Storage.

Wet markets don't only sell fresh produce, meat and fish. There are usually stalls selling dried goods, noodles and other items as well as general stalls that sell everything from shower curtains to the paper money burnt at funerals. If you can't find what you're looking for then ask the stallholders as I've always found them very eager to help.

Wet markets are all over the island but some of the most

Wet markets may be overwhelming at first, but shopping at one is the simplest way to cut your grocery bill. They may be smelly and crowded but they also have the freshest produce at the lowest prices!

popular are Tekka in Little India, Empress Market on Farrer Road, and the Tiong Bahru market. If you want to know where the market closest to you is, either ask a Singaporean or ask an experienced helper. Trading hours vary from market to market but most open around 6 am and shut at noon; Tekka has longer trading hours. Many stalls are closed on Mondays, particularly those that sell fish.

If you're not keen on buying your meat and/or fish from a wet market, there are many specialty retailers and wholesalers throughout Singapore.

- **The Butcher** (www.thebutcher.com.sg) is an Australian butchery that currently has three outlets as well as online ordering. They sell high quality beef, lamb, chicken and pork, as well as a variety of deli items.

- **QB Foods** (www.qbfood.com.sg) is a meat wholesaler that sells both fresh and frozen meat from around the world at excellent prices. They also sell cheese, frozen goods, processed meats and deli items. You must order online and you can either have your order delivered or pick it up from their store.

- **Foodie Market Place** (225 Outram Road, 169038) is a meat and specialty food store in Tiong Bahru. It is very popular with expats for its good prices and service.
- **Fishwives** (www.thefishwives.com) sell New Zealand and Australian seafood, meat and gourmet groceries from their store at Cluny Court and also from their online store.
- **German Market Place** (609 Bukit Timah Road, 269710; www.germanmarketplace.sg) sells, as you would expect, a variety of German products.
- **Belmonte Latin Foods** (www.belmontemex.com) sell authentic Mexican goods and groceries. I can personally vouch for their salsa verde!

### Eating Organically

There isn't as much organic produce in Singapore as you may be used to but both Cold Storage and FairPrice have organic sections of both fresh and packaged products. The wet market at Tiong Bahru has one dedicated organic stall and at least one other that stocks some organic produce.

**Supernature** (www.supernature.com.sg) has shops in Forum and Paragon shopping malls, and an online store. They stock fresh produce, specialty products (gluten, dairy, wheat, egg and vegan) and a variety of other holistic goods.

### Alcohol

Let me state this plainly so that you are under no illusions—alcohol costs a lot of money in Singapore. Beer is quite reasonably priced but any other type of alcohol isn't, due to liquor excise duties on imported liquor. Alcohol is available almost anywhere, including petrol stations and convenience stores but can't be sold between 10.30 pm and 7 am. It also can't be consumed in a public place during these hours, and there are tighter restrictions around Geylang and Little India for weekends and public holidays.

Beer from all over the world is available at a wide range of outlets. Whilst you may not be able to find your favourite beer from your home country, you should be able to find something that tastes like home. Even in a basic supermarket there is Tiger beer alongside a selection of beers from Australia, Japan and Europe. There are also a number of craft beer businesses emerging, with one in a hawker centre!

If you're a wine drinker, you may well find that you drink less during your time in Singapore, given how expensive a bottle is here. The minimum price for a bottle of any type of wine starts at about $20 for a New Zealand brand, and skyrockets from there. Most supermarkets will stock a reasonable selection of popular wine labels from around the world. If you are a more discerning wine drinker, there are also specialist wine stores offering a greater variety, such as Wine Connection (wineconnection.com.sg) and the Straits Wine Company (straitswine.com). If you prefer to buy your wine in bulk then check out vendors such as Underground Wines (undergroundwines.com.sg) or Benchmark Wines (benchmarkwines.com.sg).

If you prefer spirits, then the cheapest place is the duty-free shop at the airport. In a supermarket a bottle will cost in the vicinity of $60, compared to the duty-free price of about $30. However, the duty-free shop at Changi Airport restricts each purchase to one litre of spirits, plus a litre of wine and a litre of beer.

# CHAPTER 7

# THINGS TO DO

*Life might be difficult for a while, but I would tough it out because living in a foreign country is one of those things that everyone should try at least once.*

**— David Sedaris**

Once you have successfully navigated your way through all the logistics of living in Singapore, it's time to get out and about and see what Singapore has to offer. As mentioned in Chapter 1, the best way of speeding up the inevitable bout of culture shock is to make a concerted effort to get out and about. By exploring your new country, connecting with like-minded people and establishing some new routines you'll find the settling in process much easier.

Sadly, I've heard more than one friend say that there's not much to do in Singapore after the first few weeks—it's a comment that makes steam come out of my ears. The suggestions on what to see and do in the tourist brochures may take you no more than the first few weeks, but Singapore has a great deal more to offer than just the heavily marketed attractions. I firmly believe that there's a great deal to experience and all it requires is a sense of adventure and curiosity.

## TOURIST ATTRACTIONS
### Singapore Zoo, Night Safari, River Safari and Bird Park
Singapore has some of the best zoos in the world and is home to the world's first safari park for nocturnal animals. There are four zoos, each separate from the others and featuring

Pandas Kai Kai and Jia Jia are the big drawcard at the River Safari, Singapore's most recent zoo. Hopes are high that they will eventually produce a baby panda!

different animals. All are managed by the Wildlife Reserves Singapore—check its website for the locations and opening hours (www.wrs.com.sg).

The **Singapore Zoo** features a variety of animals from different continents and several great shows, but the highlight for most people with young kids in tow is the water park. My kids will zoom past the white tigers, proboscis monkeys and elephants, and head straight to the water park.

The **Night Safari** is open only at night to showcase animals in their natural night time habitats, which makes for a dark, atmospheric experience. The animals are also more active as the temperature is (slightly) cooler. There are two ways to get around the Night Safari—by tram and by foot—and I recommend doing both as they don't cover exactly the same territory. There are also a couple of shows which are well worth seeing.

The **River Safari** is the newest addition to Singapore's zoos and, as the name suggests, it focusses upon river habitats and animals. There's a boat ride toward the end that moves you through some river habitats so that you can see the animals up close but the highlight of the park is the Giant Panda Forest exhibit which houses two giant pandas, Kai Kai and Jia Jia. Hopes are high that eventually they may produce a third panda for the exhibit!

The **Bird Park** features feathered creatures with many walk-through aviaries. There are shows throughout the day and also the option of having lunch with the parrots. There's lots of different feathered creatures to see and also a kids' water park to splash around in.

## Sentosa

Sentosa (www.sentosa.com.sg) is an island off the south coast of Singapore which markets itself as the 'The State of Fun' and is easily accessible by car, train or cable car. You could even walk over from the mainland via the Sentosa Boardwalk. Most international visitors head to Sentosa to visit Universal Studios, which is part of Resorts World Sentosa (RWS; www.rwsentosa.com). RWS also includes Adventure Cove Water Park, SEA Aquarium, as well as hotels, shops, a casino and restaurants. All of the attractions at RWS are worth visiting and you can also buy annual passes if you think you'll be a frequent visitor. As with most theme parks anywhere in the world, the queues can be very long on weekends and public holidays, so if possible visit during the week. Universal Studios also allows you to skip the queues by paying extra for a Fast Pass, which is well worth it during peak times. My kids love the water slides at Adventure Cove Water Park and floating past the sting rays and dolphins on the lazy river is a real treat.

Away from RWS, Sentosa has lots of other things to offer. The southern shore is dotted with beach-side restaurants, bars and beach clubs as well as adrenalin activities like I-Fly, Mega Zip, Skyline Luge, and Wavehouse. If you're less of a thrill seeker you could opt for Underwater

Bumboats are not called bumboats because you sit in them on your bum! The word derives from the Dutch word for a canoe 'boomschuit', which translates as 'tree boat'.

The Marina Bay Sands integrated resort is one of Singapore's newest icons.

World, a cable car ride, a Segway tour or just soak up the rays at any of the beach clubs.

Those interested in Singapore's World War II heritage should pay a visit to Fort Siloso, which has the largest collection of war memorabilia. There are also a couple of pill-boxes (look-outs) at both Siloso and Palawan beaches.

## Marina Bay and the Singapore River

Even a person with minimal interest or knowledge of architecture can't help but be impressed with **Marina Bay Sands** integrated resort! Since its opening in 2010 the hotel (www.marinabaysands.com) and its attached shopping mall, the Shoppes, have become the tourist focal point of Singapore. Unless you're staying in the hotel you won't be able to visit the iconic infinity pool on the rooftop, but visitors can pay to visit the Sky Garden to take in the views. Alternatively, for the price of a drink you can view Singapore from the bar at the other end which has no entrance charge during daylight hours. Every night at 8 pm and 9.30 pm there is a light and sound show, which features a light projection from its towers and also on a wall of water in front of the Shoppes. And the best thing is—it's FREE.

The **Singapore River** was a bustling trading hub in earlier times, with boats clogging the river around Boat Quay where the warehouses were located. Today, Boat Quay is home to restaurants and pubs. It's worthwhile taking a bumboat cruise that brings you up the river and out into the bay.

Located at the mouth of the Singapore River, the **Singapore Flyer** (www.singaporeflyer.com) is Singapore's answer to the London Eye and provides a great bird's eye view of the city as well as the sea. A complete circuit takes about thirty minutes. You can opt to have dinner, high tea

## View From The Top

With all of the skyscrapers dotted around Singapore, it should come as no surprise to learn that there are lots of places to check out the skyline.

- The Pinnacle@Duxton (www.pinnacleduxton.com.sg) is a state-of-the-art HDB building in Tanjong Pagar that is 50 storeys high with a sky-bridge running between all seven towers. The sky-bridge is open to everyone at $5 per person per entry. Payment is made using your EZ Link card (see 'Transport' in Chapter 4).

- Marina Bay Sands Skypark Observation Deck (www.marinabaysands.com) costs $23 for adults and provides great views of the city.

- ION Sky (www.ionorchard.com) is a FREE observation floor on the 56th floor of the ION building on Orchard Road. From there, you can see 360° views of the cityscape.

- For bars with a view, consider visiting CÉ LA VI at Marina Bay Sands, One Altitude at 1 Raffles Place, or the Lantern Bar at the Fullerton Bay Hotel.

or cocktails while taking in the view.

**Gardens By The Bay** (www.gardensbythebay.com.sg) opened in 2012 on reclaimed land next to the Marina Bay Sands integrated resort. It has proved a popular destination for both tourists and locals. The outdoor gardens are well tended and the Super Trees are a beautiful sight when they are lit up at night. There are two indoor gardens—the Flower Dome and the Cloud Forest—that have an admission fee but the rest of the gardens, including a great water park and children's park, are free.

**Marina Barrage** (www.pub.gov.sg/marina) is located across the mouth of the Marina Channel. The dam keeps seawater out of Marina Bay and has created the largest freshwater reservoir in Singapore. The grassy area on top of the building is popular with families for kite-flying in the evening, as its one of the few places with enough of a breeze. The area around Marina Bay has also become home to a family of otters in recent years, so keep an eye out for them!

## The Istana

On many public holidays in Singapore the Istana (istana. gov.sg) is open to the public. Situated along Orchard Road near Plaza Singapura, the Istana is the official residence and office of the President of Singapore. Designed by architect John Frederick Adolphus McNair, the Istana was built entirely by convict labour as a residence for the British Governor. When Singapore established self-rule in 1959 the British turned the building and grounds over to the Singapore Government.

On select public holidays the public can visit the grounds and the buildings for a minimal cost (currently $2). Guided tours are also conducted for an additional cost and there are a variety of cultural performances and entertainment throughout the day. On the first Sunday of each month at 6pm there is also a ceremonial changing of the guards at the gates of the Istana which is a free event

## CULTURE, ARTS AND HERITAGE

### Museums and Galleries

Singapore has a wide selection of museums and galleries that cover a range of topics. Admission to the National Museums is free for Singaporeans and Permanent Residents. For foreign visitors, the admission prices are very affordable; check the websites below for the latest prices. Below is a list of national museums:

- The **National Museum of Singapore** (93 Stamford Road, 178897; www.nationalmuseum.sg) is the oldest museum in Singapore and explores the history of the country in both permanent and temporary exhibits. It's housed in a stunning colonial-era building with a modern extension located just in front of Fort

Canning Park. The permanent galleries received a full makeover in 2015 and the museum also features temporary exhibits, all with a focus on Singaporean history. This is a terrific place to learn the basics of Singapore's history.

- **Asian Civilisations Museum** (1 Empress Place, 179555; www.acm.org.sg) is located along the Singapore River and houses exhibitions focussed on Asian culture and civilisations.
- **Peranakan Museum** (39 Armenian St, 179941; www.perankanmuseum.org.sg) is dedicated to the history, culture and traditions of the Peranakans. Sometimes called the Straits Chinese, Peranakan people are descendants of Chinese immigrants who married Malay traders and locals.
- **Singapore Art Museum** (71 Bras Basah Rd, 189555; www.singaporeartmuseum.sg) houses the contemporary art collection of Singapore with many large-scale works on display from the Asian region.
- The **National Gallery Singapore** (1 Saint Andrew's Road, 178957; www.nationalgallery.sg) opened in November 2015 and houses the largest collection of Southeast Asian art in the world.

The National University of Singapore (NUS) has a museum housing several collections primarily focused on Southeast Asian history and culture. In 2015 NUS opened **Lee Kong Chian Natural History Museum** (2 Conservatory Drive, 117377; www.lkcnhm.nus.edu.sg), which is dedicated to all things found in nature including dinosaur skeletons.

NUS also conducts tours of **Baba House**, a restored Peranakan ancestral home at 157 Neil Road, 088883. Visits are by appointment only and you will need to sign up in advance for a tour; check the website for details (www.nus. edu.sg/cfa/about_us/getting_to_us.php#babahouse).

The visual arts scene is burgeoning throughout Singapore, with the government investing more funds into galleries, art storage and other artistic endeavours. Along with the Singapore Art Museum and National Gallery, there is a wide choice of galleries including the better known ones at **Gillman Barracks** (9 Lock Rd, 108937; www.gillmanbarracks.com) and **Goodman Arts Centre** (90 Goodman Rd, 439053; www.goodmanartscentre.sg). All focus on different styles of visual arts.

The Singapore Biennale (www.singaporebiennale.org) and the Singapore Art Fair (www.singapore-art-fair.com) are staged in alternate years and take place across a number of different venues throughout Singapore. If you're interested in buying some Singapore art, then the annual Affordable Art Fair (www.affordableartfair.com/Singapore) may be a good place to look. The exhibition features lots of different styles of art pieces and is held in November.

If you're interested in war and history, there are several museums that focus upon various aspects of World War II.

- **Changi Museum** (1000 Upper Changi Rd N, 507707; www.changimuseum.sg) focuses on the experiences of civilian internees and POW's during World War II, and features reproductions of the Changi Murals and the Changi Chapel.

- **The Former Ford Factory** (351 Upper Bukit Timah Road, 588192; www.nas.gov.sg/formerfordfactory) tells the story of the struggles of the local population throughout the Japanese Occupation of 1942 to 1945, and is housed in the same building where the surrender papers were signed. The museum closed in February 2016 for renovation, which is expected to take a year.

- **Reflections at Bukit Chandu** (31-K Pepys Road 118458; www.nhb.gov.sg/museums/reflections-at-bukit-chandu) is located on the hill where one of the final battles was fought before Singapore fell to the Japanese. It tells the story of the Malay Regiment before and during the war.

- The **Battlebox at Fort Canning** (2 Cox Terrace, 179622 within Fort Canning Park; www.battlebox.com.sg) is the underground bunker that was the Allied command centre prior to the fall of Singapore. It has recently been refurbished and there are regular guided tours.

---

### Friends of the Museums

The Friends of the Museums (FOM) run training programmes for those interested in becoming museum docents. Docents are volunteers who are trained to conduct tours or offer information to museum visitors. It's a great way to learn more about Asian history and culture and well as mix with like-minded people.

The FOM also runs a lecture series called Monday Morning Lecture at the Asian Civilisations Museum. The topics and speakers vary each week and cover lots of interesting information from the history of Singapore. Check www.fom.sg for more details.

---

## Ethnic Enclaves

One of the things I love about Singapore is that you can get onto the MRT under a modern skyscraper, travel a few stations and reappear in what at times seems like a whole new country. Chinatown, Kampong Glam and Little India are the traditional areas of the three major ethnicities and retain their own individuality that reflects their heritage.

**Chinatown** is a few narrow streets of shophouses which now host an array of trinket shops but it still has a Chinese vibe, especially during traditional Chinese festivals. The Chinatown Heritage Centre (48 Pagoda Street, 059207; www.chinatownheritagecentre.com.sg) is dedicated to the story of the early Chinese settlers of Singapore. Recently refurbished, it features the re-creation of a crowded shophouse that shows how hard life was in old Singapore.

**Kampong Glam** is the area around Arab Street that has been home to the Malays for hundreds of years. Housed in the former place of the Sultan, the Malay Heritage Centre (85 Sultan Gate, 198501; www.malayheritage.org.sg) has exhibits dedicated to the culture and history of the Malay people. Nearby, at the end of Bussorah Street, is the Sultan Mosque, which is open to visitors (appropriate dress required; robes are available at the counter). There are lots of restaurants in the area as well as small boutique shops along Arab Street and Haji Lane.

**Little India** is, in the words of an Indian friend, "more traditionally Indian than India". The Indian Heritage Centre (5 Campbell Lane, 209924; www.indianheritage.org.sg) opened in mid-2015 and focuses on the heritage of Indians in Singapore. The permanent exhibition traces the history of Indians living in Singapore from the pre-colonial era until today. There are some great interactive displays that will appeal to kids, too. Along Serangoon Road lies a few Hindu temples. The whole area is especially great to visit during Deepavali celebrations in October, when Serangoon Road is festooned with lights and there are lots of markets. My daughters love getting henna tattoos and then wandering through the Aladdin's Cave that is Mustafa Centre, a 24-hour shopping mall on 145 Syed Alwi Road, 207704.

Ernest Zacharevic, the artist behind Penang's famous murals, has painted several large-scale works in Singapore in recent years. These add to a developing street art culture with many HDB void decks and other public spaces featuring a growing number of public art pieces.

I've noticed during my four years in Singapore that public art pieces have been appearing more and more often. Whilst you won't find any graffiti here, there are lots of sculptures and murals that, I believe, have added a welcome edginess to the country. Ernest Zacharevic, the Lithuanian street artist who painted Penang's iconic murals, has created several public artworks in recent years. If you're keen to see his work head to the corner of Victoria Street and Jalan Pisang. My kids particularly love the mural that uses real metal shopping trolleys! Also, many of the void decks of HDB buildings have been transformed with colourful murals by talented local artists in the past couple of years. Sculptures can also be found in lots of public spaces, particularly along the Singapore River and in the CBD area.

## THEATRE AND FILM

For theatre-goers Singapore offers a good selection of stage shows, including both mainstream and more experimental offerings. Popular international stage shows often play limited seasons at **Marina Bay Sands** (www.marinabaysands.com), whilst Esplanade Theatres on the Bay (www.esplanade.

com) has a great programme of music, opera, drama and comedy by both local and international performers. There are also many, smaller theatre groups operating throughout Singapore that perform in different languages, so there is always something happening to suit theatre-goers. If you're into stand-up comedy, **The Comedy Club Asia** (www. thecomedyclub.asia) has regular stand-up gigs featuring local and overseas comedians. The best place to keep up-to-date with performing arts is to head to the **Time Out** website (www.timeout.com/Singapore).

## Opera

There are two types of opera performed in Singapore: Western and Chinese or wayang. For the former, the **Singapore Lyric Opera** (www.singaporeopera.com.sg) usually perform a couple of different works a year. They also hold an annual

free 'Opera in the Park' at the Botanic Gardens, aimed at increasing the popularity of opera in Singapore. This is a great way to get a dose of culture while relaxing on your picnic rug! *Wayang* is Chinese street opera. The performers are recognisable by their heavy but beautiful make-up and elaborate costumes. The works are usually performed in a Chinese dialect (either Cantonese, Hokkien, or Teochew) and accompanied by traditional Chinese instruments. If you don't speak the language it can be a little overwhelming! If you are eager to watch a *wayang* performance the **Chinese Theatre Circle** (www.ctcopera.com) holds regular performances throughout the year at the Chinese Tea House on Smith Street, Chinatown. They even hold courses if you are keen to learn how to perform yourself!

## Literary Arts

The local literary arts scene is thriving. Literature is written in all four major languages across a variety of genres and most bookstores have a well-stocked section of Singaporean literature, as does the National Library Board (NLB; www.nlb.gov.sg) has a terrific library network around the island. Whilst membership is free for locals and permanent residents, foreigners will need to pay an annual membership of $55. An NLB membership gives you borrowing privileges at every branch as well as borrowing of e-books for your smartphone, tablet or e-reader. Most branches have a well-stocked children's section and my kids love the fake tree growing out of the centre of the children's area in the Central branch on Victoria Street!

The annual **Singapore Writer's Festival** (www.singaporewritersfestival.com) is, rightfully, dominated by the region's literary talents. It usually runs in late-October until early November and has a wide range of workshops and events for all age and interest groups.

## Cinema and Film

Singapore has a number of cinema chains, including **Golden Village** (www.gv.com. sg), **Shaw** (www.shaw.sg) and **Cathay Cineleisure** (www. cathaycineplexes.com.sg), that screen new-release movies in all of the four major languages. Each chain publishes their screening times online and will also advise what language the movie is shown in and which (if any) subtitles are used.

One word of warning about visiting Singapore's movie cinemas—dress warmly! I'm not sure why but movie cinemas seem to set their air-conditioning to 'arctic' and I've shivered through more than one movie. Take a sweater or, better still, a blanket.

If you prefer independent movies then there are a few arthouse movie theatres around such as **The Substation** (www.substation.org), **The Arts House Screening Room** (www.theartshouse.sg) and **Sinema Old School** (www.sinema.sg). If you're a Bollywood fan then both **Rex Cinemas** (www.rexcinemas.com.sg) and **Bombay Talkies**

### Film Classifications

The Board of Film Censors (BFC) are responsible for classifying all films and videos released in Singapore. All films are classified into one of six age-appropriate ratings:

- G—General. Suitable for all ages.
- PG—Parental Guidance. Suitable for all ages but parents should guide their children.
- PG13—Parental Guidance. Suitable for persons older than 13 but parental supervision is advised for those under 13.
- NC16—No Children under 16. Suitable for those aged 16 and above.
- M18—Mature 18. Suitable for people aged 18 and over.
- R21—Restricted 21. Suitable for adults aged 21 and over.

(www.in-movienetwork.com) show movies in both Indian and Tamil.

It seems that with each passing year there are a greater number of Singaporean films being released. Most films won't make it to the screens of the big cineplexes but the Singapore International Film Festival (www.sgiff.com), which is held annually in November/December, is a great way to see local films.

## Censorship

In order to maintain a harmonious society that is free of racial, political and religious persecution, the Singapore Government, via the Media Development Authority (MDA), audits and censors (if necessary) media and the arts. This requires all play scripts to be submitted for approval before they can be staged; films are classified, and there are strict guidelines for free-to-air television. Before moving here I had been told that many movies screened were so heavily cut due to violence or nudity that they didn't make sense, but that hasn't proven to be true. Whilst all pornography is banned the movie 'Fifty Shades of Grey' was screened in movie theatres uncut, although it did receive an R21 rating which required all viewers to be over 21. Occasionally whilst watching television something of a sexual nature may be blurred out but it doesn't really impact upon the show, in my opinion.

In Singapore the internet is subject to the government's broadcasting laws, which means that your ISP will restrict access to some websites. If you attempt to access one of these websites (which are typically pornography websites) a notice from the MDA will be displayed advising that the site is blocked as it contravenes the broadcasting laws of Singapore.

## Saint Jack

In 1973, Paul Theroux wrote *Saint Jack*, a fictional novel set in Singapore during the 1950s and 60s. It features booze, blackmail, prostitution, triads and most other vices you can think to name—which contrasts completely with today's Singapore! In 1978 Peter Bogdanovich made a film of Theroux's book, which is still the only Hollywood film to be entirely shot in Singapore. Bogdanovich felt that given the book's subject matter The Ministry of Culture would never grant him a permit to film *Saint Jack* here, so he devised a second script for a tame romantic story called *Jack of Hearts* and had approval granted. The charade continued for the entire film with not even all of the cast and crew in on the rouse. When the movie was released it was immediately banned in Singapore due to its nudity and themes and the ban was only lifted in 2006. In the same year, Ben Slater wrote a book about the filming of Saint Jack called *Kinda Hot: the Making of Saint Jack in Singapore*, in which he discusses the intricacies of covertly filming a movie in Singapore. Today the strength of both the book and the movie of *Saint Jack* lies in the glimpse of a Singapore that has since disappeared.

# THE GREAT OUTDOORS

Despite being home to many skyscrapers and buildings, Singapore has an abundance of green spaces, which surprises a lot of visitors who expect to only find a concrete jungle.

## National parks and reserves

Singapore is host to a number of different national parks and reserves which are all managed by the National Parks Board (Nparks). You can find an abundance of information on their website (www.nparks.gov.sg), but below are a few of the highlights:

- **Macritchie Reservoir** is a favourite place for runners, who pound around the 11km loop which circles the reservoir. It's not just for runners, though, it's a lovely place for a walk in the jungle and home to the Tree Top Walk, a 250m-long suspension bridge between the two highest points in the area that provides a view of the jungle from above. There's usually some monkeys hanging about, so be mindful to not get too close as they are wild. You should also avoid having food visible as they may snatch it from you.

- **Singapore Botanic Gardens**, established over 150 years ago, spans 74 hectares within a five-minute walk from Orchard Road and is a popular place for tourists, expats and locals who enjoy strolling around the gardens as well as attending the various exercise classes that are held there. A highlight is the National Orchid Garden which houses over 1,000 species of orchids. There are regular free concerts at the stage area near the lake, so keep an eye out for upcoming events (www.sbg.org.sg).

- **Sungei Buloh Wetlands** sits on 220 hectares in the far north of Singapore. It's a great place to see a variety of bird and animal life in their natural habitats. The best time to visit is early morning when the animals are at the most active. It's a nature photographer's and bird watcher's paradise! You can expect to see crabs, mudskippers, monitor lizards, crocodiles, butterflies, otters and many different types of birds. The centre runs guided tours in both English and Mandarin and the theatre shows educational films regularly.

- **Bukit Timah Nature Reserve** has undergone extensive restoration works. Bukit Timah is the highest peak in Singapore at 163 metres high. It may also be the only tallest peak in any country of the world I will ever climb! There are a series of walking and mountain bike tracks throughout the reserve, some of which join up with the nearby Dairy Farm and Central Catchment reserves. The main route to the top is usually pretty busy with many locals regularly power walking up the steep slope. The car park is often a good place to see macaque monkeys who like to hang out around the garbage area on the lookout for food.

- The **Southern Ridges** is the park connector that joins Mount Faber Park, Telok Blangah Hill Park, HortPark, Kent Ridge Park and Labrador Nature Reserve, creating a 10km stretch of parks in the south of Singapore. Some of the highlights are the pedestrian bridge called Henderson Waves, and the Forest and Canopy Walks through the forest. Ideal for a jog, picnic, family outing or birdwatching.
- **Coney Island** has not a single thing in common with its namesake in New York. Reopened in 2015 after an extended closure, the northeastern island (which is accessible by road) is home to a wide diversity of flora and fauna. Guided tours are run regularly.

## Singapore Wildlife

Despite being one of the most heavily urbanised countries in the world Singapore still has an abundance of wildlife, which has been nurtured by the government's dedication to maintaining lots of green spaces. In 2015, renowned naturalist Sir David Attenborough narrated a two-part television series on Singapore's wild animals called 'Wild City'. It showcased the variety of wildlife that exists within the urban spaces of Singapore and the animals living in the nature reserves. In recent years, the waterways around Marina Bay have become home to families of otters, which can often be spotted at dawn and dusk playing in the water. A friend even saw an otter family in a canal in Bishan during her morning run. In 2015, a private house on Sentosa lost $65,000 worth of koi

carp to a hungry otter family in a single night!

If you live close to a nature reserve you may well get the occasional visit from macaques. Whilst seeing a wild monkey is at first kind of cool they can quickly become aggressive and destructive. A good rule of thumb is to never feed a monkey! Given that Singapore was once almost entirely covered by jungle it should come as no surprise that many snakes can be found. Fortunately, they tend to stay away from populated areas but there are a variety of venomous and non-venomous snakes so always stay well clear of any snake!

The wildlife which I am most familiar with are the geckos that live in my apartment. They usually disappear when people are around but occasionally one will dash out and give me a fright. Sungei Buloh wetlands is the best place to see wildlife in a natural environment and you can expect to see crocodiles, monitor lizards, and many species of birds.

## Singapore's Islands

You probably didn't know that Singapore has over 60 man-made and natural islands off its coastline, did you? If you ever feel cabin fever from living on such a small island then, ironically, a day trip to an even smaller island might just be a balm for your soul. The largest of Singapore's islands is **Pulau Ubin**, which will give you a glimpse into the Singapore of yesteryear as life there is still lived *kampong*-style. To get to Pulau Ubin, catch a boat from Changi Point ferry terminal for a 10-minute ride over. At $3 per person each way it's a budget-friendly family day out. Once you're there you can either walk, bike or even catch a minibus shuttle around the island, and check out Chek Jawa wetlands (www.nparks. gov.sg/gardens-parks-and-nature/parks-and-nature-reserves/pulau-ubin-and-chek-jawa), the mountain bike path or just soak in the relaxed atmosphere before heading back to have a seafood meal at one of the restaurants near the jetty. You can even camp overnight but be warned that this is the jungle and I've seen black spitting cobras and wild pigs!

The other easily accessible and interesting islands are the **Southern Islands** of St John's, Sisters and Kusu Islands. St John's Island was once a quarantine station but today is a nice place for swimming in the ocean and you can also stay overnight in the cabins if you book in advance. Sisters Island Marine Park is Singapore's first marine park and the National Parks runs regular guided tours, but book early as they can be fully booked months in advance. Kusu Island means 'Tortoise Island' in Chinese and during the ninth lunar month pilgrims flock to the island to visit the Chinese Da Bo Gong Temple. You can't stay overnight on the island but day trippers can enjoy the lagoon and a picnic.

Ferries to the Southern Islands leave from Marina South Wharf and you can find information about the islands on the Sentosa website (www.sentosa.com.sg/Explore/Nature/Southern-Islands).

### The Legend of Pulau Ubin

One day three animals—a pig, an elephant and a frog—had a competition to see who could reach the shores of Johor first. Whoever didn't make it would be turned into a rock. All of the animals, including the frog, had trouble swimming across the Johor Strait. The frog stopped first and was turned into Pulau Sekudu. Both the pig and the elephant stopped near each other and were turned into Pulau Ubin. Pulau Ubin was originally separated in half by the Jelutong River, but when prawn farming became a way of life on Pulau Ubin, mud bunds were placed across the river so the two halves became a whole!

## Neighbourhood parks

The urban planners of Singapore have taken great care in providing every neighbourhood with their own parks and playgrounds, although some are so hidden that they may take you a while to discover them. My children call our closest playground "the secret playground" as it took us so long to find it! If you can't immediately spot a playground ask a local and they should be able to point you in the right direction. If you live in or near a HDB estate then you will usually find a playground and a fitness park nearby. Keep a lookout for the 'dragon playgrounds' which were built in the late 1970s and feature a dragon-shaped slide, and are a much-treasured reminder of earlier times. In larger parks you may also find a Community Garden. Similar to 'allotments' in the UK, Community Gardens are a communal space where people can grow fruit and vegetables as well as an informal community centre.

This 'dragon playground' in Toa Payoh is one of the few such playgrounds remaining in Singapore. Built in the late 1970s, these playgrounds have been mostly phased out due to safety concerns.

# VOLUNTEERING

Becoming a volunteer is a great way to engage with the local community and also give back to Singapore. Whilst Singapore may look shiny and perfect it has the same problems and issues that plague any society. So there are lots of non-government organisations who depend upon volunteers in Singapore across a range of different concerns. The elderly, the disabled, the young, the poor, the addicted, and animals all have non-governmental organisations (NGOs) looking out for their needs and keen for more volunteers. A good place to begin looking for an organisation that matches your interests and skills is **SG Cares** (www.sg/SingaporeCares) or **Giving.sg** (www.giving.sg). If you are a member of an expat group or club, ask about their volunteer programme as many have ongoing partnerships with NGOs. Some schools may also have links with some NGOs that are in need of volunteers.

# OFF THE BEATEN TRACK

I freely admit that I have a preference for heading to the lesser visited parts of Singapore as I like seeing how the locals live, and I have always found that the locals like seeing expats in the heartlands. I've never once been made to feel unwelcome and have met some interesting and lovely people. So, if you want to see a different side of Singapore than what you'll find in the tourist brochures then head to the following places:

- **Sembawang Hot Spring** is a well-hidden and little known spot. Located down a path off Gambas Avenue, and within the grounds of Sembawag Air Base, is the only hot spring in Singapore. Once upon a time the water was used to make soft drinks but is now a favourite spot for locals to soak in the mineral-rich and boiling hot water. One taxi uncle tells me that he takes some eggs with him to cook in the boiling hot water, which he sprinkles with salt and eats while his feet soak. Chairs and buckets are provided but make sure you leave your clothes on!

- **Kampong Baungkok** (aka 'The Last Kampong'; near Gerald Drive off Yio Chu Kang Road) is the last remaining traditional village (*kampong*) in Singapore. It's not a tourist attraction as people do live in the 20 or so wooden houses, but they don't mind visitors walking along the road through the village so long as they are respectful. The lane shows how life once was in Singapore and I fervently hope this quiet place is never 'redeveloped'.

- **Bird Singing corners**. 'Bird singing' has been a favourite past-time of Singaporean uncles for many years and there are many places across the island where uncles gather with their caged birds to listen to them sing, but also to socialise with their friends. Kebun Baru Birdsinging Club is located behind Block 159 Ang Mo Kio Avenue 5. Sunday is the best day to visit for the regular bird singing competitions!

- **Haw Par Villa** (262 Pasir Panjang Road, 118628) is often referred to as a theme park, but it's not the modern-day theme park with rollercoasters. Rather it's a park filled with statues, all of which relay Chinese myths and fables. Originally called Tiger Balm Gardens, Haw Par Villa was founded by the Aw brothers who developed Tiger Balm. Some of the statues may be too scary for young children, particularly the Ten Courts of Hell display, but entrance is free and the park will give you a good taste of Chinese folklores.

Bird-singing is a popular past-time throughout Singapore. At the Kebun Baru Birdsinging Club in Ang Mo Kio caged birds are hung atop long poles during the day and on weekends bird-singing competitions take place.

## FUN FOR CHILDREN

A lot of the things already listed are suitable for children as Singapore is a child-friendly place, but many of them aren't cheap. If you're looking for low-cost activities to do with children, here are some you could try:

- **Public swimming complexes** in Singapore are cheap. Weekend admission for a family of four will cost $6, and it's cheaper on weekdays. Jurong East Swimming Complex (21 Jurong East Street 31, 609517) has a competition pool, water park, lazy river, wave pool and three water slides. Seng Kang Swimming Complex (57 Anchorvale Road, 544964) has swimming pools, Jacuzzi and eight waterslides. All of the swimming complexes have different facilities; check opening times and admission prices on the website: www.singaporeswimming.com/pools

- The **Road Safety Community Park** (near the Big Splash complex in East Coast Park) is a free miniature traffic environment, complete with a petrol station, overpasses, roundabouts and traffic lights. It's a great place to take the kids with their bikes and scooters to burn off some energy.

- On Saturday mornings between 9 am and 11 am the **fire stations of Singapore** throw open their doors to the public for free. Kids (and adults!) can learn about how the Singapore Civil Defence Force works, watch the firemen slide down the fire pole and even use the fire hoses. More details are available on the SCDF website (www.scdf.gov.sg).

- **Somerset Skate Park** is great for older kids who want to skate or blade, and is handily located just behind Somerset MRT Station at 1 Somerset Road,

238162. Other skate parks are located at the Sports Hub, Bishan, East Coast Park, and Woodlands.

- **Jacob Ballas Children's Garden** (www.nparks.gov.sg/gardens-parks-and-nature/parks-and-nature-reserves/jacob-ballas-childrens-garden) is part of the Singapore Botanic Gardens and aimed at children. In fact, you may enter only when you have a child with you. There are lots for kids to explore including a tree house, a water play area, a maze and a sensory garden. Entrance is free.

- Every Friday night the **Science Centre Observatory** (www.science.edu.sg) holds free star-gazing from 7.45 pm until 10 pm.

- Every Saturday and Sunday from 3.30 pm to 7 pm **Castle Beach** (www.castlescanfly.com) in East Coast Park has sandcastle-making activities, with all tools supplied. Located near Lagoon Food Centre.

## Walking Tours

On first glance you could be forgiven for thinking that Singapore is a country solely looking to the future, but there is a thriving heritage movement that is preserving traditional cultures and simultaneously celebrating modern Singapore. Being a relatively flat country Singapore is an easy place to traverse on foot (apart from the sweat factor!) and there's a wide variety of walking tours to choose from.

The National Heritage Board (NHB; www.nhb.gov.sg) has an excellent series of self-guided heritage walks for different parts of Singapore, which focus not just on the well-known areas but also on the lesser visited heartlands. The NHB offer guided tours at a variety of locations throughout the year, especially during the annual Heritage Fest in May and the anniversary of the fall of Singapore in February.

A variety of companies also offer guided walking tours, which cover most of the popular areas like Chinatown, Little India and Kampong Glam. A couple focuses on less well-known sides of Singaporean life, while others focus upon food. Check out Singapore Walks (www.journeys.com.sg), Footprints (www.singaporefootprints.com), the Betel Box (www.betelboxtours.com), and Indie Singapore (www.indiesingapore.com).

## SPORTS

Despite the heat there are lots of different sporting activities in Singapore. If you have a favourite sport, rest assured that it's highly likely you'll find it here. There are even a couple of ice-skating rinks! The easiest way to find a sporting group is to search the Internet or ask around.

Generally, most expats tend to stick to the sports that they are familiar with from their home countries. As such there are cricket matches, any kind of football you can imagine (soccer, American football, rugby, Australian Rules), netball, basketball, field hockey, tennis and the like. For fitness enthusiasts, there is a thriving industry offering boot camps, running groups, yoga classes and personal trainers that can be found across the island.

If you are a water sports enthusiast then there are a wide variety of sports, although the only real surf you'll find is the artificial wave on Sentosa. Many different places offer lessons or equipment for kayaking, canoeing, and stand-up paddle boarding. There are many dragon boat clubs throughout Singapore, with several regattas and a national championship held annually.

For keen recreational cyclists, there are lots of cycling routes. NParks has created several trails that range from 20–40km to meet the needs of cyclists. The park connectors are also an excellent place to cycle. If you prefer mountain biking, then the mountain park trails at Dairy Farm Nature Park are a great place to get dirty, as is Pulau Ubin. If you don't own your own bike, you can hire one from the kiosks located along both the Eastern Coastal Loop and the North Eastern Riverine Loop. There are also several bike hire shops in East Coast Park. Visit the NParks website (www.nparks. gov.sg) for more information on each trail.

One way of meeting more locals is to take up a sport that is played predominantly by locals. Both badminton and table tennis are popular sports with Singaporeans, with lots of lessons and competitions being run at the local Community Centres. There are several sports, such as wushu, *silat* and *sepak takraw*, that are not widely practised outside of Asia that may be interesting choices if you're keen to take up a new sport. Both *wushu* and *silat* are martial arts, whilst *sepak takraw* is similar to volleyball except the 'ball' is kicked with the feet. *Tai chi* is another popular Asian sport, which uses slow, fluid movements to build strength and maintain health. I've often seen a *tai chi* variation in Bishan Park which is involves balancing a ball on a racket (called *rouli*), which sounds easy but actually requires great skill and control.

If you're after low-cost organised sports, a great place to start is the ActiveSG website (www.myactivesg.com).

## Mahjong

If you are after a less energetic hobby that is uniquely Asian then learning to play *mahjong* may be a good option. *Mahjong* originated in China and is played by up to four players using 144 tiles that look a little like dominoes. A friend here says that one of her strongest childhood memories is sitting under the *mahjong* table and listening to the click-clack of the tiles.

ActiveSG is a portal to the various government sports and fitness activities across the island, including swimming complexes, sports complexes, exercise classes and very affordable gyms. Two additional good places to look are the Sports Hub and the Community Centres. The Sports Hub (sportshub.com.sg) is at the National Stadium which opened in 2014, and offers many low-cost and free activities for all ages. The People's Association run a network of Community Centres island-wide that offer a huge range of sports, hobbies and classes. Not only will they cost you very little but they are also terrific places to meet Singaporeans.

If you are more of a sports spectator than a participant, you'll find lots of events throughout the year to watch. The biggest spectator sport on the calendar is the Formula 1 Grand Prix (see Other Major Events later on in this chapter), which is held around a street-circuit at Marina Bay each September. The national football (or soccer) league is called the S League which has 10 teams that vie for the championship each November. The National Stadium's Sports Hub has regular events that are open to spectators throughout the year.

## Expatriate Clubs and Groups

Finding your tribe is an integral part to feeling at home in Singapore and joining a group or a club may help with this. There are many groups that are based upon nationalities, such as the American Women's Association (AWA) and ANZA (Australian and New Zealand Association) but they are open to everyone, regardless of nationality. These groups usually run a variety of social and sporting events as well as organising different interest groups such as book clubs and mah-jong groups. They also organise tours and talks on various aspects of Singapore history and culture.

There are also several country clubs to join, if you have the cash! Fees are steep but they do give you access to some great recreational facilities such as swimming pools, exercise classes and the like (refer to Resources for a list).

Another avenue for making friends and socialising are places of worship. There are a wide variety of churches, mosques and synagogues throughout Singapore which are happy to welcome newcomers (refer to Resources for a list).

# NIGHTLIFE

Singapore doesn't have quite the same type of nightlife as other parts of Southeast Asia; however, it does have a thriving bar and nightclub culture. There are bars with views, bars that require passwords, bars with no cocktail menu, outdoor bars, and indoor bars. What all bars have in common are the prices. As mentioned in Chapter 6, alcohol is expensive in Singapore, so a night out will inevitably cost a fair bit. If you're keen for a big night but want more value for your money then look out for 'free flow' events. A 'free flow' night is where you pay an upfront fee and can drink and/or eat as much as you can during a set time period. These usually happen midweek and are firmly targeted at the 'Expat Wife' market.

The two longest standing nightclubs in Singapore are Zouk (17 Jiak Kim Street, 169420) and Brix at the Grand Hyatt Singapore (10 Scotts Road, 228211). If you're after a night out but don't know where to begin then one suggestion is to head to popular areas like Club Street and Clarke Quay where there is always a good night-time crowd. The beach clubs on Sentosa are also popular nightspots.

# SHOPPING

Singapore has been known as a shopping mecca for several decades but if you're expecting to find the cheap, counterfeit products you find throughout most of Asia then you're out of luck. Singapore does not allow counterfeit goods to be sold but you can still find cheap, unbranded goods. What Singapore does excel in is a mix of brands from both Western and Asian countries, which makes it a unique place to shop. New shopping malls are continually being opened and current ones are often refurbished, so if you're a shopaholic there's usually a new mall to visit. Malls are not merely shopping

centres as many have waterparks, dog parks, libraries, synthetic ice rinks, and restaurants run by celebrity chefs!

The glitzy shopping malls used to be found mostly along Orchard Road but can now be found all over the island, so rest assured that wherever you live you will not be too far from away from your next shopping trip. Orchard Road is still the premium shopping strip and where you'll find all of the international prestige brands. Many of the Orchard Road malls are connected by underground walkways that allow you to move from one to another without seeing daylight.

Depending upon your home culture it may take you some time to adjust to shopping hours in Singapore, as most will not open until 11 am (although a few open around 10 am). Supermarkets and banks tend to open earlier, but the majority of shops have trading hours of 10.30 am until 10.30 pm

For grocery/
food shopping
please refer to
Chapter 6:
Food.

seven days per week. You may not be able to shop in the morning but you can shop every night of the week! The only time most shops are closed is during Chinese New Year so shopping can almost be a year-round activity, should you so wish. If you want the shops to yourself then I recommend shopping from 10.30 am on a weekday as all shopping malls tend to be very crowded on weekends.

Cash, debit and credit cards are accepted at most places. The electronic funds transfer programme is called NETS, so if you're wishing to pay using your debit card tell the cashier "NETS, please". Bargaining is not generally done if the product has a price-tag, but you can always try your luck if there isn't a price tag. Don't be surprised, though, if the answer is "cannot, *lah*!". If you do want to find a bargain then you need to head away from Orchard Road and into the heartlands. As a general rule, the fewer expats and tourists you see, the lower the price will be.

There are a plethora of shops in Singapore but if you need to buy clothes and/or shoes be warned that most retailers do not cater for larger sizes. A size 12 in the UK/Australia (10 in US, 42 in Europe) is the upper end of the clothing sizes for women in most Asian retailers, but fortunately there has been a recent influx on Western retailers that sell clothes designed to fit Western bodies. As a woman who wears a size 42 shoe I can attest to the difficulty of trying to find footwear to fit larger feet with most retailers only stocking up to a size 40. I have no remedy for this other than to advise that if you find shoes that fit you buy several!

The following list comprises some of the most popular shopping malls in Singapore and what you can expect to find there.

## Orchard Road

- **Tanglin Mall**, 163 Tanglin Road.
  www.tanglinmall.com.sg
  Tanglin Mall is often referred to as the 'Expat Mall' as
  it caters mainly for expat tastes. The clothes and the
  shoes are bigger, as are the prices. There's a good
  range of different clothing, shoe and homewares stores
  as well as a well-stocked supermarket in the basement.

- **Forum**, 583 Orchard Road.
  http://forumtheshoppingmall.com.sg
  There's a large Toys 'R Us store here as well as
  numerous stores for children's shoes and clothing.
  The office tower houses lots of specialist services.

- **Paragon**, 290 Orchard Road.
  www.paragon.com.sg
  The Paragon is one of the glitziest malls on Orchard
  Road with an abundance of high-end fashion outlets, as
  well as Marks and Spencer and the Metro department
  store. There's a supermarket in the basement and an
  excellent assortment of eating places throughout.

- **ION**, 2 Orchard Turn.
  www.ionorchard.com/en
  ION is host to eight floors of shopping, with most of it
  under street level so be prepared to get lost! ION has a
  mix of high-fashion stores, mid-range labels (Top Shop,
  H&M), and the basement is home to the Japanese
  $2-store, Daiso. It also has a large food court and a
  Marketplace supermarket.

- **Ngee Ann City**, 391 Orchard Road.
  www.ngeeanncity.com.sg
  Ngee Ann City is best known for the Japanese
  department store Takashimiya and the largest bookstore

in Singapore, Kinokinuya. The mall has a good selection of both Western and Asian brands, and several beauty choices such as Sephora and Bath & Body Works. The Cold Storage supermarket at the bottom of Takashimiya carries an extensive range of Japanese goods.

- **Orchard Gateway**, 277 Orchard Road.
www.orchardgateway.sg
Orchard Gateway is the newest mall on Orchard Road and home to the country's newest (and coolest) public library. It includes a good mix of a variety of retail stores. There is a library on the third floor.

- **Plaza Singapura**, 68 Orchard Road.
www.plazasingapura.com.sg/en
Plaza Singapura is a long-time Orchard Road favourite and a personal favourite of mine. It was originally opened in 1975 and renovated and expanded in 2013. It has a good variety of mid-range stores including Marks and Spencer, Mothercare, Uniqlo, Gap as well as Australian sewing and homewares store, Spotlight. On the top level, there's a cineplex, and in the basement, a supermarket and the art supply store, Art Friend.

### Central

- **Vivocity**, 1 HarbourFront Walk.
www.vivocity.com.sg
Vivo, as it's commonly called, is located above Harbourfront MRT. It is home to Tangs department store and Giant Hypermarket. It has an excellent choice of mid-range stores, a Cineplex, a rooftop waterpark and an excellent selection of places to eat.

- **Marina Bay Shoppes**, 10 Bayfront Ave.
www.marinabaysands.com/shopping.html

The Marina Bay Sands Shoppes are just in front of the iconic Singapore landmark building Marina Bay Sands and it has attracted lots of shoppers away from Orchard Road since it opened in 2010. It is home to many high-end designer stores, celebrity chef restaurants, a theatre, a casino, a synthetic ice-skating rink and a large, busy food court. As if that isn't enough, you can also take a gondola ride along a man-made canal.

- **Great World City**, 1 Kim Seng Promenade. (www.greatworldcity.com.sg)
  Great World City takes its name from a former amusement park that was once in the same location. Today's Great World City features a large supermarket, a cineplex, a number of mid-range clothing shops, children's stores, an indoor playcentre and many cafes.

## Elsewhere

- **NEX**, 23 Serangoon Central.
  www.nex.com.sg
  NEX is in the central area of Serangoon and is the largest mall in the north-east part of Singapore. It has an extensive choice of mid-range shops from clothing, shoes, homewares and beauty services. It is rather unique in that it has two different supermarket chains. The rooftop hosts a dog park with its own pet-friendly lift and escalators, as well as a kids' waterpark. There's a wide choice of places to eat, a branch of the public library and the Serangoon MRT station is in the basement.

- **IMM**, 2 Jurong East Street 21.
  www.imm.sg/en
  IMM features over 50 outlet stores across a range of

shops that offer impressive savings that you won't find shopping in regular malls. Its disadvantage is that it's not near an MRT line, but the potential bargains are worth the bus ride.

- **Cluny Court**, 501 Bukit Timah Road. www.clunycourt.com.sg

  Cluny Court is a small, boutique shopping centre aimed squarely at the expat market. It houses a number of small women's and children's apparel, and homewares stores. There's also a supermarket and a few different cafes to dine at, many of which are occupied during the day by people who've been exploring the Botanic Gardens across the road. It is right next to Botanic MRT station as well as along a number of bus routes.

Not all shopping in Singapore has to be done in a neon-lit shopping centres as there are many other places to shop, which will also give you a chance to view the different styles of living in Singapore.

- **Arab Street:** The areas around Arab Street are a mix of fabric/tailor, rug, and trinket stores all with a Middle Eastern touch. Haji Lane, which runs parallel to Arab Street has some very interesting and unique stores that have a more urban feel than a shopping mall.
- **Little India:** Serangoon Road and its surrounds provide a good place to explore the sights and smells of Little India. An Indian friend says this area is more Indian than Mumbai! No trip to Little India is complete without a visit to Mustafa's, a department store opened 24/7. It is so vast that just when you think you've seen all you will stumble upon a new section. Whilst it may be a sensory overload on your first visit it is worthwhile persisting as

the prices here are some of the best in Singapore.

- **Chinatown:** Despite being clogged with an over-abundance of shops selling generic jewellery and trinkets, Chinatown retains its Chinese ambiance, thanks to the beautiful shophouses that line the streets. During the lead-up to Chinese New Year the already crowded streets are lined by market stalls selling all manner of CNY goodies. If you're looking for Singapore souvenirs to send back to your home country Chinatown is an excellent place to find them. Temple Street has a couple of kitchenware stores that sell well-priced basic goods.
- **Tiong Bahru:** The oldest public housing estate in Singapore has experienced a surge in popularity in the past few years due to the number of hip cafes, bookstores, and other interesting shops. In the market expats shop side-by-side with locals for fresh produce and other items.

Tiong Bahru features Singapore's oldest public housing built by the Singapore Improvement Trust (SIT) in the 1930s. Today the area is home to hip cafes and restaurants as well as a wet market and food centre.

- **Dempsey:** The old army barracks at Dempsey have been repurposed into a variety of furniture stores with an emphasis on Asian antique and reproduction furniture. If you find shopping in the non-air-conditioned stores tiring you can head to any number of restaurants, cafes and bars to refuel before continuing your shopping.

Some Singapore malls tend to specialise in a particular demographic or niche, so which mall you visit depends on what you're looking to buy and this may take you time to become accustomed to. This is a brief guide of which mall to head to for specific items:

- **Sports:** For sporting goods check out Velocity (438 Thomson Rd), Queensway Shopping Centre (1 Queensway), or Peninsula Shopping Centre (3 Coleman Street).
- **Music:** Bras Basah Complex (231 Bain Street) has an excellent choice of music shops, as well as great stationery, craft, and book stores.
- **Children's goods:** Forum Shopping Centre (583 Orchard Road), United Square (101 Thomson Rd).
- **Furniture:** Tan Boon Liat building (315 Outram Rd) has lots of furniture shops. IKEA has outlets at Alexandra and Tampines.
- **Electrical devices and computers:** Sim Lim Square (1 Rochor Canal Road). If you're after electrical appliances, head to Best Denki, Courts, Harvey Norman or Mustafa.

# TRAVEL

When you have lived your whole life in Australia where it takes a minimum of four hours by flight to reach another country, the travel opportunities from Singapore can make you feel like a kid in a candy store—spoilt for choice. Or, perhaps this was just me? The novelty of being able to take a day trip to another country still blows my mind, even after five years!

As Singapore is so centrally located to the rest of Southeast Asia, it's possible to take a weekend trip to just about any SE Asian country. Malaysia is the easiest destination, with many people opting to drive or catch a bus to Johor Bahru (JB) for a day of shopping. Clearing Customs is relatively easy but you can encounter long queues at both checkpoints, and if you're travelling over a public holiday then you will undoubtedly encounter LONGER queues. If you're heading beyond JB to either Malacca or Kuala Lumpur, then the easiest way to travel is on a coach, most of which are very comfortable and some have onboard entertainment and toilets. It is also possible to fly to Kuala Lumpur, which takes slightly beyond one hour.

The Indonesian islands of Bintan and Batam are both just a short ferry ride from Singapore and are a very popular destination for people looking for a quick weekend break. Bintan Island has lots of resorts and hotels to choose from including The Banyan Tree as well as Club Med. Batam has a good selection of hotels in the city as well as beach resorts.

If the idea of travelling by car, bus or boat doesn't appeal then you can choose to fly just about anywhere in Asia from Changi International Airport. With the increased number of budget carriers travel is more affordable than ever before. Whether your travel dream is lazing on a tropical island (Phuket, Langkawi, Bali), snow-skiing (Japan, Europe), exploring ancient ruins (Cambodia, Yogyakarta) or climbing a mountain (Kota Kinabalu, Nepal) all are possible holiday destinations from Singapore.

## FESTIVALS

Singapore likes to celebrate and you'll find some sort of a celebration for just about everything, including many days particular to certain countries due to the numbers of foreigners that make Singapore home. On top of the official Singapore public holidays and their related celebrations there are also events for Australia Day, Waitangi Day (NZ), Independence Day (USA), Remembrance Day (Commonwealth countries), St. Patrick's Day (Ireland), Bastille Day (France), Holi (India) and Valentine's Day to name but a few!

### Singapore Gazetted Public Holidays

Singapore has 11 gazetted public holidays each year for a variety of traditions and celebrations. Singapore's public holidays reflect its multicultural heritage as they span Hindu, Islamic, Christian and Chinese traditions as well as national events. This acknowledgement and celebration of Singapore's diversity is one thing I truly love about Singapore.

### New Year's Day—January 1

Celebrations start with the traditional New Year's Eve party, a countdown and fireworks usually centred at Marina Bay. Celebrations vary from year-to-year but there's usually a concert that begins in the late afternoon and carries on through until midnight. There are also lots of other places to celebrate, with almost every bar, restaurant and hotel having their own functions to welcome the New Year.

## Chinese New Year—January/February

As Singapore's population is almost 80 per cent Chinese, it should be no surprise that Chinese New Year (CNY) is the biggest celebration of the year. So important is CNY to Singapore the shops actually close! Unlike January 1, which is an excuse to party with friends, CNY is focussed on family and tradition. Chinese New Year is also known as Lunar New Year because the timing of the New Year is dictated by the moon's cycle. Whilst the holiday lasts for 15 days only the first two day are gazetted public holidays in Singapore.

The preparations for CNY start long before the actual day, with houses being thoroughly cleaned and food prepared. By cleaning the house Chinese people believe that all of the bad luck is washed away and they begin the New Year free from any bad luck that may have been hanging around.

The eve of CNY is when families gather to enjoy a reunion dinner. Traditionally, the reunion dinner was held at the home of the most senior family member but this now varies from family to family. Sometimes it's held at the home of the family member with the biggest house, while other families will opt to celebrate at a restaurant. At the reunion dinner, family members will usually kneel before their elders and say blessings for the coming year. The elders will then give their unmarried younger relatives *ang pows* (red packets). Offerings will also be made to departed ancestors. In Chinese families (but not Peranakan) the hosts will give two mandarin oranges to each guest as a symbol of prosperity. At some time during the night, the front door will be opened for a

## CNY Goodies

Singaporeans love food and Chinese New Year is particularly food-centred. Many people will indulge in variety of delicious goodies that are made especially for CNY.

Sweets are a very popular CNY treat and heading the list are pineapple tarts. These are a small short-crust pastry filled with pineapple jam. It's difficult to only eat one of these! Other popular sweets are *kueh bangkit* (coconut biscuit),and *kueh baulu* (small sponge cake). Much of what is eaten during CNY is chosen not just for its deliciousness but also for its symbolism. Candy/sweets/lollies are believed to sweeten the year ahead. Chocolates are often in the shape of coins, which symbolises wealth and prosperity, while groundnuts are believed to mean good health and long life.

Lots of savoury dishes are also eaten during CNY. If you see a very long queue around Chinatown in the lead-up to CNY it may very well be for *bak kwa*: thinly sliced barbecued meat (usually pork). Prawn rolls, Chinese sausage, and waxed duck are other favoured treats.

Reunion dinners are typically lavish and will feature a large number of dishes. It's believed that by eating well and plentifully the coming year will also be full and plentiful. As such it's common to see abalone, fish, prawns, and other expensive ingredients on the table. One highlight of CNYs culinary offerings is *yu sheng*. This is a salad made up of thin strips of raw salmon, white radish, red capsicum, and many other ingredients. All are believed to be auspicious. The dish is usually placed in the middle of the table and the family use chopsticks to mix the ingredients by tossing them in the air. The higher they toss the better the coming year will be!

short period to welcome in the new year. Some families will consult a geomancer (*feng shui* master) to find out the most auspicious time for this to happen.

The first 15 days of Chinese New Year are traditionally a time for visiting family and friends. People will take delicious CNY goodies with them to give to their hosts, and also ang pows. If there has been a death in the family leading up to CNY the family will not traditionally visit their family and friends during this time, although they will welcome visitors into their own house.

There are many public events during CNY. Most are in Chinatown and the best website for keeping up-to-date with all the Chinese festivals throughout the year is the Chinatown Festivals site (www.chinatownfestivals.sg). The first big CNY event is the ceremony that turns on the lights throughout Chinatown. The light-up usually takes place two weeks before CNY and the lights remain on until the end of the festival four weeks later. There are also nightly stage performances in Kreta Ayer Square that feature dance, song and storytelling. Many of the streets in Chinatown will also be lined with market stalls selling traditional CNY goods during this time.

The Chingay Parade and the River Hongbao are two large public events that happen over the Chinese New Year period. The Chingay Parade has been staged since the early 1970s and is the largest float parade in Asia. Staged at the Pit Buildings at Marina Bay, the parade celebrates all ethnicities and cultures, not just the Chinese. Smaller but no less colourful parades are held throughout the island in the month following CNY. The River Hongbao is staged on the floating platform on Marina Bay and features large, brightly lit lanterns. There are also food stalls selling traditional CNY dishes and carnival rides. If you haven't been invited to a reunion dinner on the eve of CNY then a visit to the River Hongbao that night is a great way to avoid that crowds who will descend upon it the next evening!

Another highlight of CNY in Singapore is the lion dances that seem to appear out of nowhere at any time of the day or night. One of my favourite CNY sights is groups of lion dancers sitting in the back of open trucks festooned with flags. A lion dance is performed by a team of two people, plus a group of drummers. The lion will usually dance around the house/property/business they are at and this is believed to bring it prosperity in the forthcoming year. The property

Lion dances are performed over the Chinese New Year period all over Singapore, in both private and public spaces. They are believed to bring good luck and prosperity, and are a joyous riot of noise, colour and movement.

or business owner will then present the lion with a platter of green, leafy vegetables, mandarin oranges and an ang pow as payment. The lion will then settle down to 'eat' the food, which usually involves tearing it up and throwing it. This makes all the kids squeal!

The mandarin oranges are peeled and the segments are used to make the Chinese character for the coming year's animal sign in the Chinese zodiac. At my condo, the lion takes pity on the expats and writes the character (using the segments) in English!

### Good Friday—March/April

Good Friday is a Christian Easter celebration that marks the day Jesus Christ died. As with many religious festivals Easter has no fixed calendar date but is aligned with the March equinox and usually falls in late March or early April. The Christian churches of Singapore hold services to mark the occasion. Easter Sunday, which marks the day Jesus Christ is believed to have risen from the dead and ascended to heaven, is traditionally celebrated by the giving of Easter eggs and chocolate. I've noticed during my time in Singapore that there are many more stockists of Easter chocolate and sweets now, with most large supermarkets carrying a good selection. There are also a few places that organise an Easter Egg hunt for children on Easter Sunday, including the expatriate clubs.

### Vesak Day—April/May

Vesak Day celebrates the birth, enlightenment and death of Buddha and is the most important holiday for Buddhists. Vesak Day is usually in April or May, depending on when the full moon occurs. Buddhist temples will be decorated with flowers and lanterns. Buddhists will attend temple to offer prayers and offerings of flowers and candles, and to meditate. Some Buddhists release caged birds as a symbol of liberation for Vesak Day. In the lead up to the day there is also a candlelit procession, with light passing from one person to another to show the passing on of Buddha's teachings. Non-Buddhists are free to join in the celebrations.

## Labour Day—May 1

Like many countries around the world Singapore celebrates Labour Day on May 1, which is often referred to as May Day. The day is a day of solidarity for workers; in Singapore it is marked by a rally and a speech delivered by the Prime Minister.

## Hari Raya Puasa—not fixed

Hari Raya Puasa is an Islamic celebration which marks the end of the holy month of fasting known as Ramadan, and is traditionally a time for reflection, kindness and charity. *Hari raya* means 'grand day to rejoice' in Malay, while *puasa* means 'fasting' so the day is literally a day of celebrating the end of the fast! It's the most important celebration of the Islamic year. Ramadan is held during the ninth month of the Islamic calendar, and is dictated by the moon's cycle. As the moon cycle varies slightly depending upon geographical location there are sometimes slightly different timings for Ramadan from place to place. In times past Ramadan would only begin when the full moon was cited but the timings are now forecast in advance. In Singapore Ramadan and prayer timings are co-ordinated by Majilis Ugama Islam Singapura (MUIS; www.muis.gov.sg) and announced on their website and in the media.

For the thirty days leading up to Hari Raya Puasa, Muslims fast from sun-up to sundown as a way of marking the month that the Qu'ran was presented to Mohammed. Fasting is one of the Five Pillars of Islam as prescribed in the Qu'ran. By fasting Muslim people believe that they cleanse their soul and also develop self-discipline. Not all Muslim people fast. Exceptions are made for the elderly, the sick, women who are pregnant or breastfeeding and pre-pubescent children. Menstruating women do not need to fast, but instead repay these days later. Muslim people will also abstain from sex, smoking and sinful speech during Ramadan.

Before the sun rises during Ramadan someone in each Islamic household will wake up and prepare a meal, called *sahur*, which is the last meal eaten until the sun sets. No food or drink can be taken during the fast. The meal eaten to break the fast is called *iftar*, and is usually shared with the whole family which helps to strengthen familial bonds. One popular food for breaking the fast are dates, chosen as they are high in sugar and easy to digest.

In line with the rest of the year Muslim people continue to pray five times a day during Ramadan. This is called *salat*. An additional evening prayer called *isyak* is held after the fast is broken and this will include lengthier readings from the Qu'ran than usual.

In the days leading up to Hari Raya Puasa houses will be cleaned, new clothes and household goods will be purchased, and delicious food will be prepared. Many companies will give their employees a half-day off work on the eve of Hari Raya. Houses and apartments will also be lit with fairy lights to signal to family and friends that visitors are welcome.

On the morning of Hari Raya Puasa, Muslims will attend

mosque for the traditional Hari Raya prayers. Afterwards they will say to each other "*Selamat Hari Raya! Maaf zahir batin!*", which means "Happy Hari Raya! I seek forgiveness from you!" Forgiveness is an important part of Hari Raya with old grievances and disagreements forgiven.

After morning prayers Muslim people will spend the day visiting family and friends. Some may also visit their departed loved one's graves. For children the day is full of excitement as many will receive *duet raya*, which is a green envelope with some money inside. These are also given to elder family members as a way of showing respect. A friend tells me that as long as you are still at school you should receive a green envelope, but as soon as you start working you are expected to give, not receive!

Many Muslim people will prepare or buy Raya treats to share with their friends and family. These are also given out to neighbours, even those who are not Muslim. Neighbours will repay the generosity during either Chinese New Year or Deepavali. Some of the traditional treats are *kueh tart* (pineapple tart), *kek lapis prune* (prune layer cake) and *kuih makmur* (prosperity cookie). Many of these treats are also popular Chinese New Year treats.

Although many Malay Muslims dress in Western clothes most of the time, most take the opportunity to wear traditional Malay clothing for Hari Raya Puasa as a way of honouring their heritage. Ladies wear either a *baju kurung* or a *baju kebaya*. Both feature a long skirt worn with either a long, loose shirt or a kebaya which is a loose jacket. Men wear the traditional baju Melaya that has two parts: a long shirt with a stand-up collar, and loose pants. Men often also wear the *songket samping* (waist cloth) and *songkok* (brimless hat). In recent years, a trend of families all dressed in the same colour has emerged in Singapore, with many bazaars catering for this. Dressing in the same colour is a way of showing the unity of the family, which is an important aspect of Hari Raya.

There are several Ramadan bazaars that appear in Singapore during Ramadan: at Kampong Glam, Geylang Serai, Tampines and Woodlands. These bazaars are very festive with the neighbouring streets decorated with lights. Inside the bazaar there are all manner of stalls, including clothing, jewellery, homewares and food. After the sun sets the food stalls get very busy as people break their fasts with a variety of delicious dishes. At Geylang Serai bazaar one of the favourite foods is the Ramly burger, which looks just like a cheese burger except the meat patty has been wrapped in a thin omelette. Other popular options are Middle Eastern *shwarma* (similar to a taco) and many different fried foods. Visiting a Ramadan bazaar is a great way to enjoy the festivities and non-Muslims are very welcome. If you aren't a fan of crowds then you may want to visit early in the Ramadan period as the closer the end of Ramadan gets the more crowded the bazaar will be!

### National Day—August 9

Singapore's National Day on August 9 marks the day in 1965 when Singapore gained its independence from Malaysia. The highlight of the day is the National Day Parade (NDP) that takes place on The Float in Marina Bay (moving to the National Stadium from 2016). It begins with formal proceedings that include military parades, before moving onto a colourful and fun concert. Tickets to the parade are free but are only available for Singaporeans and Permanent Residents. However, don't despair as there are practice runs

The National Day Parade takes place on August 9 each year and commemorates the day Singapore achieved Independence in 1965. The parade is a true show of patriotism with march pasts, songs, fireworks and a fly-past by choppers and jets.

every Saturday night for about six weeks before the actual day. From any spot around Marina Bay you'll be able to see the jets fly past, the national flag draped from the bottom of a chopper, the gun salute, and once the sun goes down you can watch the fireworks. If you prefer to stay at home and avoid the crowds you can watch the NDP on television. Each year there is also a song specially written for the National Day celebrations by popular Singaporean singers/songwriters.

### Hari Raya Haji—not fixed

Hari Raya Haji is an Islamic festival that is also known as the 'Festival of Sacrifice' as it commemorates Prophet Ibrahim's dedication to Allah by his willingness to sacrifice his son. Allah swapped Ibrahim's son with a sheep to repay Ibrahim's devotion. It also has a dual purpose of celebrating the end of Hajj, which is the pilgrimage of Muslims to Mecca. The pilgrimage to Mecca is the fifth pillar of Islam. All Muslims with the physical ability and the financial means are expected to make the journey once in their lifetime.

Muslims will observe Hari Raya Haji by attending the mosque for prayers. After prayers, male volunteers will then sacrifice a sheep, goat or cow and the meat will then be distributed amongst the Muslim community. The cattle are provided by attendees of the mosque and the animals are sacrificed to honour Ibrahim's sacrifice to Allah. By sharing the meat with the entire community, the festival helps to draw the community closer to each other. After the traditional practices of the day have been observed, people will visit family. A Muslim friend says that Hari Raya Hajj is a much more low-key celebration than Hari Raya Puasa.

## Deepavali—October/November

Deepavali is a Hindu festival held between mid-October and mid-November each year. The origins of Deepavali are disputed but most interpretations are of good triumphing over evil, and this is represented by the lights which decorate Indian houses during Deepavali. As such the celebration is often called the 'Festival of Lights'. In the lead-up to Deepavali, Indian people prepare by cleaning their houses, buying new clothes, and preparing food to share with family and friends. The doorway of houses are often decorated with *rangoli*, which are intricate patterns made using coloured rice powder and grains.

The public celebrations of Deepavali centre around Little India, with Serangoon Road decorated with colourful lights, and many bazaars are set up throughout the area. The light-up remains for a month and is a beautiful sight to behold. The bazaars sell a variety of goods and food, and are a great way to experience Deepavali.

Saint Andrew's Cathedral is Singapore's largest cathedral. The Anglican cathedral is located near City Hall MRT station in the heart of the city.

## Christmas—December 25

Christmas Day falls on December 25 each year and marks the birth of Jesus Christ. Christian places of worship will hold a variety of church services over this period and will often include carolling and charitable works. (See Chapter 10 for a list of Places of Worship).

The heart of Christmas festivities in Singapore is Orchard Road, and a stroll from one end to the other to take in the multitude of Christmas displays has quickly become one of my family's favourite Christmas traditions. Almost every shopping centre along Orchard Road, from Tanglin Mall to Plaza Singapura, will be decorated and there will be lights twinkling above the road and from every tree along the way. It really is a lovely sight. The highlight for many children is playing in the 'snow' at Tanglin Mall: although, as this is the tropics, it's not real snow but bubble foam. If you are keen to continue the tradition of an annual photo of your children with Santa both Tanglin Mall and Great World City usually have a photo stall.

A large percentage of the expat population disappears from Singapore over the Christmas period, returning either to their home country or taking the opportunity to travel, but there are still lots of dining options for Christmas Day itself if you're not planning on cooking. Many of the five-star hotels have Christmas lunch buffets that include entertainment for the kids. If you're not interested in Christmas celebrations then you can always go shopping!

## Chinese Celebrations
### Qing Ming

Qing Ming is also known as Tomb-Sweeping Day. Traditionally it is the day when people tend to the graves of their deceased loved ones. Debris around the graves is removed, foliage trimmed and offerings made. With traditional burials becoming fewer, families now also pay their respects at the various columbariums throughout Singapore.

### Hungry Ghosts Festival

During the seventh month of the Chinese calendar (usually in August), Taoist Chinese believe that the Gates of Hell open and spirits return to roam the earth. You'll know it's Hungry Ghost time when you spot people burning paper money and paper items on the footpaths. You may also notice burning joss sticks and plates of food left out. These are all to appease the spirits. There are also shows performed during Hungry Ghosts, with stages and tents erected throughout the island. These shows are to entertain the spirits and feature wayang or getai performances as well as more modern forms of performance. Anyone is welcome to watch a Hungry Ghost show but whatever you do, do not sit in the front row as this is left empty for the ghosts!

## Mid-Autumn Festival

The Mid-Autumn Festival (also called the Lantern Festival) is held on the 15th day of the 8th month of the Chinese calendar. This usually falls from mid-September to mid-October. The origins of the festival are disputed but are believed to have been a commemoration for Chang'e. Legend has it that her husband obtained an elixir of immortality, which his apprentice tried to force Chang'e to give to him. Chang'e then drank the elixir to prevent it from falling into the wrong hands.

In Singapore the festival is celebrated by hanging lanterns and eating mooncakes. Mooncakes are a round pastry which has a tasty filling. The traditional fillings are red bean and lotus paste, but they are now made with a variety of fillings.

During Mid-Autumn Festival most shopping malls will have stalls set up selling mooncakes. Many businesses will also give mooncakes to their staff.

As with most Chinese festivals in Singapore, Chinatown is the best place to take part in the Mid-Autumn Festival. The streets are strung with lanterns and performances take place regularly.

## Malay Celebrations
### Maulud Nabi
This 12th day of the third month of the Islamic year marks the birthday of the Prophet Muhammad. Special prayers are said in the mosque to mark the occasion. 'Birthday parties' may also be held for underprivileged children and this reflects one of the core values of Islam.

### Awal Muharram
Awal Murraham celebrates the first day of the Islamic New Year. Unlike New Year's Day and Chinese New Year, this is a quiet celebration and Muslims usually attend religious lectures and prayers.

### Israk and Mikraj
This celebration marks the ascension of the Prophet Muhammad. It is usually observed by attending public lectures.

## Indian Celebrations
The Indian community in Singapore have four main annual festivities throughout the year. Only Deepavali is given a public holiday as it is the one of the biggest Hindu festivals, but the other festivities are equally enjoyable! The timing of

these festivals are in accordance with the Tamil calendar which typically begins on April 14 every year.

## Tamil New Year

Tamil New Year falls on April 14 and is celebrated by offering *pongal* (see below) at the family altar and by a vegetarian feast with family. The New Year is also welcomed by wearing a new outfit of clothes and a Tamil friend assures me that even his bedsheet will be new!

## Pongal

*Pongal* is the Harvest Festival which usually falls in mid-January each year. *Pongal* is particularly important in rural India where livelihoods depend upon a good harvest. Although Singaporean Indians do not face the same circumstances, they continue to celebrate *Pongal* by decorating the front door-step with sugar cane and preparing pongal. *Pongal* is a sugared rice dish that is usually prepared in the traditional manner over a charcoal stove using clay pots. The pot will bubble over, which represents abundance and prosperity. The dish is how the festival came to be named!

The *Pongal* celebration spans four days of festivities. The first is dedicated to the home, the second to the cows that toil in the fields, and the third to young girls of the area. The final day is dedicated to community building, with younger people seeking the blessings of their elders. On this day offerings will be made at temples and employers may give gifts to their workers.

The best place to take part in Pongal festivals is, as you may expect, in Little India. The Sri Srinivasa Perumal Temple on Serangoon Road hosts a range of different celebrations and performances over the days of the festival. If you have children they may enjoy feeding the cows and goats, who will have their horns colourfully painted for the occasion! The area around Campbell Lane will also house stalls selling outfits, trinkets and henna painting to mark the occasion.

## Thaipusam

Thaipusam is a Hindu festival which is celebrated by the Tamil community and is usually celebrated in January or February. Thaipusam commemorates Parvati giving Murugana a *vel* (spear) so he could vanquish the evil demon Soorapadman. Whilst the procession is the part of the festival that most people are familiar with the families will also make *pongal* (a sweet rice dish) and present is an offering to the gods at the family altar.

The Singapore Thaipusam procession begins at the Sri Srinivasa Perumal Temple on Serangoon Road and ends 4 km later at the Sri Thendayuthapani Temple in Tank Road. Each participant will usually carry with them along the route a burden. These range anywhere from a small pot of milk to a *kavadi* which is a large metal structure that can be pierced into the skin. Whilst it may sound quite gruesome I've attended Thaipusam several times and have found it be a joyous and beautiful celebration. Onlookers can watch from anywhere along the procession route and are also able to go inside both temples, but ensure you are modestly dressed (shoulders and knees covered) and remove your shoes.

## Other Major Events
### Formula 1 Grand Prix—mid-September

If you're a motorsports enthusiast then the Formula 1 Grand Prix (www.singaporegp.sg) is designed for you. On a Sunday

night in mid-September, Formula 1 cars take to a street circuit around Marina Bay, with the sound carrying for miles! Tourists flock from all over the world and any room or office with a view of the track is highly valued. 'Early bird' tickets go on sale around Easter and this is the best time to buy cheap tickets, but it's usually not too difficult to get a ticket provided you have enough cash. If you're not into motorsports there are always concerts after the race, featuring some of the biggest entertainment names in the world (and usually at least one from the 1980s). The downside of the race is that the area around Marina Bay can be difficult to access for a week or so before and after the actual race, with many streets blocked off in preparation. Unless you absolutely have to visit that part of Singapore, it is best to stay clear.

### Great Singapore Sale—May to July

Sure, it's not technically a celebration but given the prominence of shopping in Singapore I consider it a suitable event to mention. End-May to end-July is Singapore's sale season, which is organised by Singapore Retailers Association as a way of attracting more tourists to the island. Most retailers get in on the action and offer a wide selection of discounted stock. It's not the only time of the year that goods are discounted but it is a good time to find a bargain!

## Notable events

- World Gourmet Summit (www.worldgourmetsummit.com) is heaven for foodies. Held every April, the event is a festival devoted to food and drink.
- Singapore International Festival of Arts (www.sifa.sg) is held biennially in August and showcases a broad range of arts.
- The Pink Dot (www.pinkdot.sg) event is held in Hong Lim Park each June to show support and love for the LGBT community.
- Singapore Writer's Festival is devoted to all things literary (www.singaporewritersfestival.com). Held each October/November in various locations around the Arts area the festival features local and international literary talents across a range of genres.
- Singapore Night Festival (www.brasbasahbugis.sg/snfportal) is held every August around the Bras Basah/Bugis area. It features the work of artists who use light to make beautiful works of art.
- Singapore Air Show (www.singaporeairshow.com) is held every two years at Changi Exhibition Centre and features all things aeronautical.

# CHAPTER 8

# LANGUAGES

*If you are bilingual, you have binocular vision...
you see the world in 3-D.*

**— Lee Kuan Yew, 1977 speech to parliament**

Singapore is a multi-lingual nation, with four official languages: English, Mandarin, Malay and Tamil. These languages reflect the history and multi-cultural heritage of Singapore. English is the main language of Singapore and is the language of government and the business community. Malay is the native language of the region. Mandarin is the official language of the majority ethnic group. Tamil is the language spoken by the majority of Singaporean Indians. Whilst there might be four official languages, perhaps the most popular 'language' amongst Singaporeans is Singlish. Singlish is a unique mix of all the official languages with a bit of slang thrown in for good measure (see Singlish in this chapter).

Singapore's public schools have a bilingual policy. Classes are instructed in English, but all students must study a second language of either Mandarin, Malay or Tamil—this is known as the students' mother tongue. I find it a little ironic that a student's mother tongue is dependent upon the ethnic background of his/her father, not mother! This means that almost all Singaporeans who were born after Independence in 1965 are at least bilingual, but many people speak three or more languages or dialects (such as Cantonese and Hokkien). As someone who has only mastered a single language (and being Australian some would argue that I've yet to master English!) this is something of which I am very envious. The ability to speak more than one language is a great skill in today's modern world.

If you are interested in learning any of the local languages then a good place to start is the People's Association Community Centres. They run regular language classes and prices are very reasonable.

## ENGLISH

English is the language of business and administration. The decision to choose English as the main language is due, partly, to the British colonial history of Singapore. During colonial times, government and administrative business was conducted in English and by the time Britain cut Singapore's colonial ties it had become the accepted language of government, commerce and administration.

However, English is much more than a hangover from colonial times. The pioneers of independent Singapore foresaw that choosing English as the main official language would create greater opportunities in the business world. In modern Asia, Singapore has the highest proficiency of English amongst all Asian countries, which makes it attractive as a place of business for other international English-speaking businesses. Thirdly, in 1965, the then Prime Minister Lee Kuan Yew felt that by choosing either Chinese, Malay or Tamil as the main language the other ethnicities would be alienated. So by choosing English the three main ethnicities were treated equally.

If you are an English speaker then knowing you are relocating to a country that has English as an official language is a huge comfort. However, every country has their own unique accent and linguistic quirks, and Singapore is no different. If you're like me it may take you some time to tune your ear to the Singaporean accent. Particularly during my first couple of years living in Singapore the combination of Singlish, the speaker's accent, and my Australian accent has made for some rather difficult conversations at times. Over time I have learnt to modify my own speech to be better understood and to also better understand the Singaporean accent.

A government initiative called the 'Speak Good English Movement' was developed in 2000. It aims to promote the use of grammatically correct English, and discourages some of the common grammatical errors of Singaporeans. The government was concerned about how Singaporean's English usage was judged by others, particularly within the international business community. Signage and advertisements are used by the movement to try and correct some of the common grammatical errors. The movement's success is debateable, with many opponents feeling that the quirks of Singaporean English are part of the national identity.

## SINGLISH

Singlish is much more than Singaporean English. It's primarily English but is mixed with words and phrases from Malay, Chinese and Tamil, and a few home-grown peculiarities to boot. I will admit that when we first moved to Singapore I found Singlish a little irritating. This may be because Singlish is stripped down, lacking many of the words and phrases that pepper standard English. For example, a question asking for permission such as "Could I borrow your phone?" is 'shortened' to "Can borrow phone?" This can make Singlish somewhat jarring at first. However, it is important for expats to be able to understand and use some Singlish. You can easily get by in Singapore without learning a word of Mandarin,

Tamil or Malay but a basic understanding of some common Singlish terms is a necessity! Like it or not, familiarity with Singlish will make life in Singapore a whole lot easier. As an example, when confirming appointments I have a tendency to respond with a full sentence such as "Yes, thank you, 3.45 pm on Wednesday afternoon is perfect'. Until I got to grips with Singlish this would routinely get me a 'eh?' response from the person I was speaking to. All that is actually required is a simple 'Yes, can'. If I say that I am immediately understood and we both go happily about our days.

Many of the grammatical rules that apply to English don't apply to Singlish as it draws many of its grammatical structures from Chinese. Whilst these breaks with standard English may grate on you when your first arrive please keep in mind that Singlish is a spoken language, not a written one. The important thing is that the message is communicated from the speaker to the listener, so hard and fast grammar rules are not required. Rather than become bogged down trying to understand the grammatical rules of Singlish it's easier to just learn a few key words and phrases.

Whilst it's not overly important to have a thorough understanding of all the grammatical differences between English and Singlish, the following points will help you come to better grips with Singlish.

- Using the past tense is optional. For example, 'What happen?' is perfectly acceptable. There is no need for the –ed on 'happen' as there would be in standard English. Sometimes 'already' or 'liao' at the end of a phrase is used to indicate past tense: 'You go shop already?' or 'You go market liao?'. This sentence structure is a direct derivative of Chinese sentence structures.

| WORD/PHRASE | MEANING |
| --- | --- |
| *Ang moh* | Literally meaning 'red hair' but used to describe Caucasian people. |
| Aunty | Any older lady. This an affectionate term but it can also imply that the person is unstylish. |
| Blur | An adjective that means confused or stupid. 'He so blur!' |
| Can/cannot | This broadly means 'yes/no' but 'can/cannot' can also be asked as a question. For example, 'Thursday. Can?' and the answer is either 'can' or cannot'. |
| *Chope* | A verb that means to reserve your seat in a food centre by placing something (tissues, umbrella) on the table. |
| *Goondu* | Idiot or fool. |
| *Kiasi* | Literally meaning 'afraid of dying'; an adjective meaning 'cowardly'. |
| *Kiasu* | Afraid of losing out to other people. |
| *Lah* | This is often tacked onto the end of phrases or sentences and is used to give a phrase emphasis. 'Can *lah*!' means as 'Yes, definitely!" |
| Revert | To reply. This is used particularly in emails: 'I will revert back to you on that tomorrow'. |
| *Shiok* | Describes a feeling of pleasure. 'This food is *shiok*!' means "This food is amazing!" |
| Slippers | Flip-flops or thongs (that are worn on the feet). |
| Talk cock | To speak nonsense. |
| Uncle | Any older man. As with 'aunty' it is a term of affection but also implies a lack of style. |
| *Wah!* | An exclamation word. |

- Plurals are generally unnecessary. 'Why two car?' gets the message across just as effectively as if 'car' had been given its 's'. This varies across speakers but there is no clear distinction made between the plural and singular forms of nouns. Uncountable nouns such as "furniture" and "clothing" may take on a plural form such as "furnitures" and "clothings". This may be related to the fact that there are no plural/singular forms for Chinese nouns.
- When emphasising a word in a sentence that word is typically repeated several times, such as in 'take the big-big one'. Big-big is used instead of an adjective like 'very'.
- When asking questions usually a word or two is added on to the end of sentence, such as 'can', 'cannot', and 'or not'. 'You want chicken rice, or not?'

## It's all about the Discourse Particles!

A discourse particle is a word that is typically tagged onto the end of a sentence. Without the discourse particle the sentence is still grammatically correct, but the discourse particle changes the emphasis of the sentence. Discourse particles are common in Chinese languages and dialects and as Singlish borrows heavily from these it's worthwhile understanding how they work. Listed below is a loose hierarchy of popular discourse particles, from mildest to most expressive:

- *Lah*
- *Leh*
- *Lor*
- *Liao*

- *Ha*
- *Hor*
- *Mah*
- *Meh?*
- *Siah!*

As an example, the sentence "I can't come" changes tone depending on the discourse particle added. "I can't come *lah*" means "I really can't come"; "I can't come *lor*" is tinged with regret as it translates as "I sadly can't come"; whilst "I can't come *siah*!" expresses exasperation in "I can't believe I can't come!"

## Helpful words and phrases

For more resources on Singlish, please refer to the 'Further Reading' section of the Resource Guide.

## MANDARIN

When Mandarin was declared the official Chinese language of Singapore it was not a universally spoken language amongst the Chinese. Back then, Chinese Singaporeans spoke different languages or dialects that reflect where in China their ancestors came from. For example, one of the most popular dialects, Hokkien, originated in Fujian province in China. Other popular dialects spoken in Singapore are Teochew, Hakka, and Cantonese.

Even after Mandarin was declared an official language many Singaporean Chinese were not conversant in the language. In 1979, the government launched the Speak Mandarin Campaign, which encouraged people to move away from speaking dialects and towards Mandarin. Lee Kuan Yew felt that by speaking only in Chinese dialects, the country's Chinese population was missing out on many opportunities, and the different dialects were dividing the Chinese community. So strongly did Mr Lee feel about this that he stated "wise parents will never let their children speak dialects at all". The campaign encouraged people to stop speaking dialects at home, particularly to young children. The number of people speaking Mandarin has certainly risen but it has had the unintended effect of many young Singaporeans not sharing a common language with their grandparents who speak only dialects.

For people who have never spoken an Asian language, Mandarin can be a very difficult language to master. Indeed, Mandarin is usually ranked as one of the hardest languages to master, with some studies saying that 2,200 hours of classroom study are required for mastery. In comparison, a language like Spanish or French takes about 600 classroom hours to reach a decent level of proficiency. Mandarin mastery is difficult as Chinese grammar patterns and structures are quite different from English ones (e.g. verbs have no tense), and Chinese characters are largely pictorial and not phonetic. That is, they can't be decoded by sounding out letters as can be done with other languages. Rather, you have to memorise the pronunciation of each character—in short, Mandarin is reliant on memory. Rote learning is the only way to come to grips with it! An added complexity is that Mandarin is a tonal language with four tones or pitch contours. The same sound said in different tones can mean different things and represent different characters. For example, *tang* can mean 'soup' (1st tone) or 'sugar' (2nd tone).

Mandarin is written only in characters, but to help people learn the language it is often taught also in *pinyin*. This is a phonetic system that transcribes Chinese characters into the Latin alphabet to aid correct pronunciation. It's important to remember that whilst *pinyin* is a very useful learning tool it's not how Mandarin is generally written. Any Mandarin writing you will see in Singapore will always be in characters.

There are two free-to-air Mandarin television channels (Channel U and 8). *Lianhe Zaobao* and *Shin Min Daily News* are both daily broadsheet newspapers written in Mandarin, and *My News* is in both English and Mandarin. Radio stations which broadcast in Mandarin include 883JiaFm (88.3), Y.E.S. 93.3FM (93.3), Capital 95.8FM (95.8) and LOVE 97.2FM (97.2).

## Helpful words and phrases

| Hello | *Ni hao* |
|---|---|
| How are you? | *Ni hao ma?* |
| Yes | *Shi de* |
| No | *Bu (shi de)* |
| Good bye | *Zai jian* |
| Thank you | *Xie xie* |

## MALAY

The Malay language holds a very important place in Singapore's history as it is the indigenous language of the region. As such Singapore's national anthem, *Majulah Singapura* (Onward Singapore), is in Malay. Malay, or Bahasa Melayu as it is more formally known, is the most commonly spoken language in the countries that surround Singapore. Both Malaysia and Brunei speak Bahasa Malay, whilst Indonesia uses Bahasa Indonesian, which shares many similarities.

Malay is a relatively easy language to learn as it is written in the Latin alphabet and has fewer grammatical rules than some languages. Of the three other national languages Malay is one which is most similar to English. As with most modern languages, words and phrases from other cultures have been incorporated into Malay. The Indian culture has had enormous influence over many aspects of Southeast Asian culture for many centuries and as such many Sanskrit words have become part of the Malay language. Other words have been drawn from all of the various countries which have influenced the Malay Peninsula including Arabic, English, Persian and Portugese.

Not only has Malay absorbed linguistic influences from other places, but many Malay words have also made their way into English. These include amok, gecko, mangosteen, sarong and satay. In Singapore you will often hear the Malay word *kampong*, which is the word for village and it refers to the traditional village based living arrangements in Singapore. Many of the street names throughout Singapore incorporate Malay into them, such as *lorong* (lane), *jalan* (walk), and *bukit* (hill).

*Berita Harian* and *Merita Minggu* are Malay language newspapers, whilst Suria is the Malay free-to-air television channel. Both Warna 94.2FM and Ria 89.7 FM are Malay language radio stations.

## Helpful words and phrases

| Hello | *Selamat pagi* (Good morning)<br>*Selamat petang* (Good afternoon)<br>*Selamat malam* (Good night) |
|---|---|
| Goodbye | *Selamat tinggal* (if you're going)<br>*Selamat jalan* (if you're staying)<br>*Sampai jumpa lagi* |

| Thank you | *Terima kasih* |
| Yes | *Ya* |
| No | *Tidak* or more informally, *tak* |
| Coffee | *Kopi* |
| Tea | *Teh* |
| Sugar | *Gula* |
| To eat | *Makan* |

## TAMIL

The Indian community comprise about 10 per cent of Singapore's population and about 60 per cent of Singaporean Indians speak Tamil. The remainder of the Indian population speak a variety of mother tongues including Hindi, Malayalam, Punjabi, Sindhi, Gujarati and Singhalese. As noted in Chapter 4, this breadth of languages is reflective of the wide range of backgrounds in Singapore's Indian population.

The use of Tamil in Singapore has declined in recent years, with many opting to speak English as their primary language. However, amongst the Tamil community and in areas of Singapore that have strong Tamil links the language is still spoken on a day-to-day basis. You are likely to hear Tamil spoken throughout the Little India area but also in the north of Singapore. Sembawang was once home to a large Tamil-speaking community, and although the area is now home to HDBs Tamil is often heard in the nearby hawker markets and temples.

Tamil is written in abugida script and has 12 vowels, 18 consonants and a special character that is neither a vowel nor a consonant. When Tamil is written it varies a lot from spoken Tamil. There are grammatical, vocabulary and pronunciation differences between the written and spoken forms which learners of the language may struggle with. In short, written Tamil is much more formal that spoken Tamil.

There is both a Tamil-language television station (Sun TV on Starhub), a radio station (Oli 96.8FM), and a daily newspaper (*Tamil Murasu*). Several of the large cinema chains screen Tamil-language movies and there are both Tamil theatre and literary works.

## Helpful words and phrases

| Hello | *Vanakkam* |
|---|---|
| Goodbye | *Poi varukiren* |
| Thank you | *Nandri* |
| Please | *Thayavu Seithu* |
| Yes | *Āmām* |
| No | *Illai* |
| How are you? | *Eppadi irukkīnga?* |

## COMMUNICATION OVERALL

You should never underestimate the importance of non-verbal communication. So much of someone's intent can be read using a person's facial expressions, body language and posture. When you relocate countries it can be difficult to read the non-verbal communication cues of the people around you, and conversely your own body language may be sending an entirely different message than what you intended. The absolute best method of communicating without words is to smile. A friend of mine who has lived as an expat in seven different countries swears that the advice 'just smile and wave' from the Penguins of Madagascar movie has got her through a lot of difficult situations. After all it's very hard to be annoyed with a person who is smiling

at you! In Singapore it's not important to get too concerned about your body language, provided you make eye contact and are pleasant.

Some complexities with communication are linked to the character traits and values have been covered in other chapters, and these include:

- Rather than responding to a question with an outright 'no' a Singaporean may say 'I will try' or 'maybe'. This is in order to not lose face. Sometimes you can reword the question so that you can receive a more helpful and definite answer.
- As social harmony is important in Singapore, losing your temper and raising your voice will not usually achieve much. It is much better to speak at a regular volume and in a calm and controlled manner.
- It's acceptable to pause before answering.

Singaporeans tend not to speak without thinking and will take a moment to think before responding. Just give the person some time to collect their thoughts and try not to prompt them.

- You will need to modify your speech so that you don't use slang from your own country as its meaning may either be lost in translation or misinterpreted.
- Small talk can often include questions which are considered very personal in other cultures, such as how much rent you pay or how much you earn. This isn't intended to be an intrusion of your privacy; rather it's showing an interest in you.

# CHAPTER 9

# WORK CULTURE

> ❛I like work: it fascinates me.
> I can sit and look at it for hours.❜

## — Jerome K. Jerome, Working Culture

Almost every person who relocates to Singapore is doing so for work, or at least for a job opportunity for a family member so understanding some aspects of Singapore's work culture is crucial. With so many multi-national corporations operating in Singapore it is very difficult to clearly define Singaporean work culture, as much is driven by the company's internal work culture. If you work for a multi-national company then your working life may well be very similar to what you experienced in your home country. Whilst if your job is with a local company you may find many distinct differences between your old and new workplaces. Even in a multi-national company there will be still be inevitable cultural differences that are due to the mix of different cultural backgrounds amongst the employees. In order to ensure that Singaporeans are not overlooked for jobs in favour of foreigners companies must employ local talent. This means that even if you are working for a large multi-national company your colleagues will come from a variety of cultural backgrounds, so understanding some of the different ways a Singaporean workplace may operate is crucial.

Firstly, hierarchy is respected throughout Asia and with this comes a reasonably strict set of etiquette. The organisational structure of a company is important with respect automatically given to those higher up the chain. Respect is shown partly by never openly questioning, contradicting or correcting a superior. Whilst in some countries this may be seen as showing initiative and drive, in Asian societies it is considered very disrespectful. If you absolutely must question your superior's judgement then it should be done in a private situation to prevent them losing face.

Singaporeans communicate in subtle and indirect ways. Whilst many expats come from cultures where being upfront and forthright is the norm when stating their opinions, this is not something that Asian people are comfortable with. One friend who manages a team of fifteen Singaporean staff members says that opinions or ideas are often suggested tentatively, rather than assertively, even when it is something the employee considers to be of great importance. This can make facilitating meetings a very different experience if you

are coming from a workplace culture where employees are encouraged and expected to voice their ideas and opinions. This means that attention needs to be paid to the non-verbal communication cues just as much as the spoken words.

One important non-spoken cue is laughter. Be mindful of mistaking laughter as just a way of expressing amusement, as in Singapore laughter can be the result of a number of different emotions. Laughter is sometimes used to mask feelings of nervousness, shyness, embarrassment or distress.

Controlling one's emotions in the workplace is very important in Singapore. Generally speaking Singaporeans keep their emotions in check and this means that outbursts of annoyance and anger are rare. Conflict is usually dealt with in private and without raised voices. As discussed before the avoidance of losing face is of utmost importance to many Singaporeans, so if there is a need to address any form of conflict or correct an employee's behaviour this should always be done in a private location. You may also find that discussing a workplace issue or point of conflict is usually a one-way conversation between a superior and their employee. The hierarchical deference that is shown to those in superior roles means that even if the person you are addressing disagrees with you vehemently they may not voice their thoughts.

Another aspect of work life in Singapore is the respect for the different cultures and traditions. This is particularly important if your role includes managing people. Managers need to be particularly aware and respectful of their staff's cultural and religious traditions and enable them to be observed. For example, Malay staff may require breaks throughout the day in order to perform their prayers or require extra leave for their religious celebrations and this needs to be taken into account when assessing leave requests.

Whilst it's important to be mindful that Singapore may have some variations with work culture Singaporeans are a very tolerant and accepting people. They are usually well-accustomed to expats and will usually not hold any faux pas against them!

## OFFICE ATTIRE

Office attire for men is generally dress pants and a long-sleeve business shirt. Even in the CBD area, it's rare to see someone wearing a complete business suit, although a suit jacket is sometimes worn to important meetings. Due to the climate neckties are rarely worn.

As is often the case, defining office wear for women is a bit trickier but relatively modest office wear is appropriate. As with any new job, if you are unsure of the company's dress standards, ask whether there are any regulations before your first day.

## WORKING HOURS

Working hours vary between companies and also between roles, but office hours are (loosely) 8 am to 5 pm. However, it is very common for people to work much longer hours than these. Very few workplaces offer flexible working arrangements, such as job sharing or work from home arrangements.

## GIFT-GIVING

There is a strong culture of workplace gift giving in most Asian countries, and Singapore is no exception. This will be particularly apparent if you work for a local company. However, the Singaporean Government have very strict anti-corruption laws so gifts should never be given to government employees or businesses. To avoid allegations of bribery it's preferable that gifts are given to a team or department, rather than an individual, and do not need to be expensive. Gifts of sweets or cakes are appropriate, but be mindful that Muslims do not drink alcohol or eat pork products and the Chinese prefer not to receive clocks or scissors. It is not customary for gifts to be opened in front of the giver. Rather, you will be thanked for your gift and it will be opened and shared later. It's also customary, particularly with the Chinese culture, to refuse a gift the first time it is offered. Do not take offence as this is the way the recipient demonstrates that they are not greedy. Simply offer the gift again and it should be accepted.

## MEETINGS

The way meetings are conducted depends on the work culture of the individual work place. Companies which are very hierarchical will have a more formal approach to meetings with staff introduced and sometimes seated according to seniority. Other companies will be more informal with these. When making introductions always bear in mind that not all Singaporeans are comfortable shaking hands. In particular, Muslim people may be uncomfortable with body contact with members of the opposite gender. The best way of deciding how to greet people is to follow their lead: if they extend a hand then it's fine to shake hands, but if they choose to smile and nod then you should follow suit. Handshakes in Asia may not be as firm as you may be used to but your hand may be held for slightly longer than you are accustomed to. Just roll with it and remember the expat mantra of 'it's not wrong, it's just different'!

Business cards are usually presented at the beginning of a meeting and the exchanging of business cards in Asia is of much more importance than in other countries. Etiquette dictates that business cards are given (and received) with both hands and with the card positioned so that the receiver can read the information. The receiver should always take a moment to read the card before either placing it in a business card holder or on the table in front of you. They should be treated with respect and not stuffed absently into a bag or briefcase and you also should not write on the card. To do so is to disrespect the person who gave it.

When arranging meetings with other companies it is usual to schedule meetings at least two weeks in advance. Details of the participants, including their names, job titles and contact details, should be given prior to the scheduled

time. Punctuality is expected and there may be minimal small talk as this can be seen by some, especially Chinese people, to be a waste of time. Don't interpret this as rudeness: it's simply a form of pragmatism.

In Singapore it's important to build a strong relationship before you can expect to close a deal. It is exceedingly rare for any binding decisions to be made in a first meeting as a relationship needs to be built first, so you will need to be patient if you are accustomed to closing a deal in the first meeting. It's very important to consider aspects of Singaporean culture in order to build strong relationships. In particular, you should avoid placing potential business partners in a position where they may lose face, and show appropriate respect to those in more senior roles.

As stated earlier much can be learnt from a person's body language and this is particularly true in business meetings. Singaporeans may not be entirely comfortable delivering a blunt 'no' and instead have a tendency to talk around the problem. Some of the non-verbal cues that may show that the meeting is steering into uncomfortable territory is the sucking in of breath, furrowed brows, fidgeting, and nervous laughter. By paying attention to these sort of messages you will be better able to control the direction of the meeting.

## EMPLOYMENT CONTRACT

Whilst both the Employment Act and the Employment of Foreign Manpower Act are the governing pieces of employment legislation for expats in Singapore, most working conditions will be outlined in the employment contracts of individual employees. This should be read and signed before you commence work and it will outline work-related issues such as salary, working hours, annual leave entitlements, sick leave entitlements, and termination details. Some contracts will also include sections relating to confidentiality, ownership of intellectual property, and any other entitlements such as health insurance. As with any contract make sure you read your employment contract thoroughly and seek legal advice if you have concerns before signing.

Whilst the Employment Act isn't applicable to all roles, as it is primarily for manual roles that pay less than $4,500 per month, it is good to know the basic entitlements particularly if you will be managing staff in Singapore. These include:

- Leave: Paid annual leave is available after three months of service. The number of annual leave days rises from a minimum of seven days the longer you stay at the one company. There are also provisions for sick leave, maternity leave, paternity leave and carer's leave. Gazetted public holidays are considered to be rest days.
- Working hours: a full-time working week is considered to be 44 hours, whilst a part-time working week is up to 30 hours. A working day can be no longer than 12 hours, unless there are extenuating circumstances.
- Minimum wage: there is no specified minimum wage.

### Dependant Passes, LTVP And Work

The work situation for accompanying spouses has been covered in Chapter 5. However, the work situation for people on a Student Pass is a little more complicated. For Singapore residents the minimum working age is 13 (although those under 16 are restricted to light duties in non-industrial roles), but Student Pass holders must be over 14 to seek employment. Working part-time during the school year is only permitted under strict criteria: the student attends one of the approved polytechnics or universities listed on the MOM website and works less than 16 hours per week. During vacation time the rules are less stringent with most students aged over 14 years who attend a listed institution (including many international schools) able to work part-time.

If you are eligible (meaning you hold DP, student pass, or a LTVP and are married to a Singapore citizen) and interested in working during your time in Singapore then you can start job-hunting. There are many ways to find a job. Many expats find work through their networks or by directly approaching companies directly or such as 3C Synergy (construction, oil and gas; www.3csynergy.com), Aegis Recruitment (www. aegis-recruitment.com.sg), and Egon Zehnder (www. egonzehnder.com). There are also many online recruitment websites that employers advertise vacancies on. Some popular ones are Contact Singapore (www.contactsingapore. sg), JobsDb (sg.jobsdb.com), and Job Street (www.jobstreet. com.sg). The *Straits Times* newspaper has a classified jobs section in the Saturday paper.

A point of note is that as of 2014 under the Fair Consideration Framework all companies must try and fill any vacant position with a Singaporean citizen before being able to hire a foreigner. This framework is designed to strengthen the Singapore core of the workforce. The Fair Consideration Framework stipulates that job advertisements should not state a preference regarding 'nationality,

You can find more information on the Fair Consideration Framework at http:// www.mom.gov.sg/ employment-practices/ fair-consideration-framework age, race, religion, language, gender, marital status or family responsibilities' but they can specify 'Singapore citizens only'. All companies must advertise each position on a government job banks website which is open only to Singapore residents for a set period of time before they can legally hire a foreigner for the position. Companies also have a set quota for the number of foreigners they can hire, so that is a factor to consider in your job search.

The interview process in Singapore may be quite different from what you are used to, particularly if you have come from a country that has strict laws about what can and can't be asked. It is not at all uncommon to be asked questions that would be deemed as too personal in many countries, such as if you intend to have (more) children or what religion you follow. It's also standard to provide a photograph with your resume.

## RUNNING A BUSINESS

Singapore is quite open to foreigners owning and operating businesses. If you are planning to move to Singapore to open a business you will need to apply for an EntrePass before you arrive. (See Chapter 5 for more information regarding the various types of work passes.)

There are five different categories of businesses in Singapore: sole proprietorship, partnership, Limited Liability Partnership (LLP), Limited Partnership (LP) and Company. Of the five only two (LLP and Company) are legal entities, which means that they can be sued in their own name and own or hold property. The best place for finding the most accurate and current information is the SME Portal website (www.smeportal.sg) which details the various advantages and disadvantages of each type of business structure.

It would be wise to seek professional help if you are intending to start any type of a business in Singapore to make certain that you have complied with all of the legal requirements. There are steep penalties for not adhering to the law so you should ensure in advance that you will be able to comply before opening the business.

### SingPass

SingPass (Singapore Personal Acess Password) is an online account management system for access to government agencies. Your SingPass will allow you to manage matters such as filing tax returns, completing your Foreign Domestic Worker training course, and starting a small business.

Once you have received your EP/DP, you are able to apply for your account at the SingPass website (www.singpass.gov.sg). Registering is quite straightforward but you will need to wait for the password to be mailed to your registered address, thus it's important that your address is up-to-date.

## Business Structures

- **Sole proprietorship:** a business owned by one person. The advantages of a sole proprietorship are that they are relatively easy and cheap to set up, however the owner is personally liable and can be sued in their own name. The business owner must be a Singapore citizen or Permanent Resident.

- **Partnership:** has two to 20 partners. As with the sole proprietorship they are quick and easy to set up but all partners will have unlimited liability for both themselves and the other partners, and can be sued in the firm's name. All partners must be Singapore citizens or hold PR status.

- **Company:** registered business entity under the Companies Act. A company can hold property in its name and members are not personally liable for debts and losses of the company. Companies have many costs and formalities involved in setting them up.

- **Limited Liability Partnership (LLP):** A blend of partnership and a company a LLP operates in much the same way as a partnership but the partners have a separate legal identity. Each individual partner is only legally liable for their debts or decisions that incur legal action. AN LLP has fewer costs and formalities than a Company.

- **Limited Partnership (LP):** an LP must have at least two partners; one general partner and one limited partner. The general partner has unlimited legal liability, while the general partner's liability is limited. An LP can not be sued or own property in its own name. An LP is reasonably quick and easy to set up.

## Sole Proprietorship

Whilst it's wise to seek professional assistance for setting up a business, many people find that operating a small business suits them perfectly during their time in Singapore so it's worth discussing this type of business in more detail. There is a large number of accompanying spouses who develop specialised small businesses and many of these are marketed directly at expats. Fairs and markets throughout the year provide a good opportunity for small businesses to sell their products, and many accompanying spouses put their skills to use in other ways, such as becoming a personal trainer.

If you have the permanent residency (PR) status, drive and initiative, starting a sole proprietorship business can be a profitable and fun experience. However, you should be aware that as a sole proprietor you are personally responsible for all debts and liabilities. This means that your personal assets are not protected and may be used to repay debts, which brings with it the chance of personal bankruptcy. Information regarding bankruptcy in Singapore can be found on the Ministry of Law website (www.mlaw.gov.sg).

In June 2016, the rules regarding sole proprietorships changed, with only Singapore citizens and PRs now eligible to become sole proprietors, as well as partnerships. If you have PR status and wish to become a sole proprietor, register the business with the Accounting and Corporate Regulatory Authority (ACRA) at their website (www.acra.gov.sg). You will need a SingPass (see overleaf) to do this but the process is usually relatively easy and costs are relatively minimal.

Unlike the other types of registered businesses a sole proprietorship is fairly easy to close. Once the business' liabilities have been settled, the business can be closed via the ACRA website. If the business is registered for GST you will also need to cancel the GST registration with the Internal Revenue Authority (IRAS).

## Registering for GST

Goods and Services Tax (GST) is a broad-based consumption tax which is applied to almost all goods and services within Singapore. Businesses operating within Singapore with a turnover in excess of $1,000,000 for four consecutive quarters must be registered for GST. For more information on GST and how to register a business for GST, visit the IRAS website (www.iras.gov.sg).

# CHAPTER 10

# FACTS AND FIGURES

> ❛Singapura, oh Singapura,
> Sunny island set in the sea.
> Singapura, oh Singapura,
> Pretty flowers bloom for you and me.❜

**— Local children's song popular
in the 1970s and 1980s**

## Official Name
Republic of Singapore

## Capital
Singapore

## Flag
Adopted in 1959, the Singapore flag has a red top half and a white lower half. The top left hand corner features a white crescent moon and five stars in a circle. The red half of the flag represents universal brotherhood and the equality of all men, while the white half represents purity and virtue. When joined together the two colours signify Singapore's goals of meritocracy (the achievement of goals and unity through virtue). The crescent moon was chosen as it represents a rising young nation, while the five stars each signify the ideals of democracy, peace, progress, justice and equality.

## National Anthem
*Majulah Singapura* (Onward Singapore)

## Time
Greenwich Mean Time +8 hours (GMT +8)

## Telephone Country Code

+65

## Internet top-level domain

.sg

## Location

1°18'N  103°51'E

## Land Area

718.3 square kilometres.

## Highest Point

Bukit Timah at 163.3 metres.

## Climate

Tropical—humid and hot with two monsoon seasons.

## Natural Resources

Deep water ports.

## Population

5.54 million (2015).

## Ethnic Groups

Chinese (74%), Malay (13%), Indian (9%), and other (4%).

## Religion

Multi-religious. Buddhism, Christianity, Islam and Hinduism are the most popularly observed faiths.

## Official Languages
English, Mandarin, Malay, Tamil.

## Government Structure
Parliamentary republic.

## Currency
Singapore Dollar (SGD; S$).

## Gross Domestic Product
$296.1 billion USD (2015).

# FAMOUS SINGAPOREANS
## Politics
- **Lee Kuan Yew** is considered to be the founding father of modern Singapore. Born in 1923, he was a student during the Japanese Occupation and afterward studied law at Cambridge. After returning to Singapore, he was instrumental in the founding of the People's Action Party (PAP) and served as Prime Minister (1959–1990), Senior Minister (1990–2004), and Minister Mentor from 2004 until his retirement in 2011. His death in 2015 was mourned widely in Singapore.
- **Lee Hsien Loong** is the current Prime Minister of Singapore. He is the eldest child of Lee Kuan Yew. Before entering politics, Mr Lee served with the Singapore Armed Forces (SAF), where he was the youngest Brigadier-General to be appointed.
- **J B Jeyaretnam** was the first Member of Parliament (MP) from an opposition party. He served from 1981–1986 as an MP and from 1997–2001 as a non-constituency MP.

- **Dr Kanwaljit Soin** was Singapore's first Nominated Member of Parliament (NMP) in 1992. Since leaving Parliament in 1996 she has worked tirelessly for women's rights.
- **Low Thia Khiang** is the leader of the Worker's Party and has been an elected MP since 1991.
- **Chiam See Tong** is Singapore's longest-serving opposition MP. He served for almost 27 years for a number of different opposition parties.
- **Goh Chok Tong** is Singapore's second Prime Minister. He served as Prime Minister from for 14 years from 1990 until 2004 and remains an MP.
- **Ong Teng Cheong** was the first directly elected President of Singapore. A qualified architect, Mr Ong served as President for six years from 1993 until 1996.
- **Chia Thye Poh** was a MP representing the Barisian Solialis (now defunct) from 1963 until 1966. In 1966 Mr Chia was detained under the Internal Security Act for allegedly being involved in pro-communist activities.

## Sport

- **Joseph Schooling** is Singapore's most successful swimmer. He represented Singapore at the 2016 London Olympics and has won medals at the Asian Games, the SEA Games and the FINA World Championships. He won his first gold medal at the 2016 Rio Olympics.
- **Fandi Ahmad** is an international soccer player, playing for the Singapore national team as well as with various European clubs. After retiring from playing Fandi became a coach and currently coaches LionsXII in the Malaysian Super League.

- **Tan Howe Liang** is Singapore's first ever Olympic medallist. He took the silver medal in the lightweight weight-lifting category at the 1960 Rome Olympic games.
- **C Kunalan** is a Singaporean athlete, who at the 1968 Mexico Olympics ran the 100 metres in 10.38 seconds. This was a national record that was not broken for another 33 years.
- **Ang Peng Siong** is a swimmer who held the world number one ranking for the 50 metre freestyle event. He is currently Swimming National Head Coach.
- **Joscelin Yeo** is a swimmer who represented Singapore at the Olympics, Commonwealth Games and Asian Games. She was also a Nominated Member of Parliament (NMP) from 2006 until 2011.

## Entertainment

- **Dick Lee** is Singapore's most prominent singer and songwriter. His career has spanned several decades and he has written several National Day songs.
- **Corinne May** is a musician, singer, and songwriter. She has released five albums and her concerts frequently sell out.
- **Jack Neo** is an actor, director and host on both television and in film. He is most widely known for his comedic roles which often involve cross-dressing.
- **Kumar** is Singapore's favourite drag queen.
- **Royston Tan** is a Singaporean film-maker known for both his short and feature-length films.
- **Stefanie Sun** is a Singaporean singer-songwriter known for her Mandopop tunes. She has sold more than 30 million records.
- **Kit Chan** is a singer and actress who performs and

records in Mandarin, Cantonese and English.

- **Jeremy Monteiro** is a jazz musician who is renowned worldwide.
- **Russel Wong** is a photographer who has photographed many Hollywood celebrities. He has staged photographic exhibitions both within Singapore and around the world.
- **Ashley Isham** is a Singaporean-born fashion designer who is currently based in London. His clothes have been worn by the British Royal Family and other celebrities.

## Literature

- **Michael Chiang** is a playwright, novelist, editor and media consultant. His play, *Army Daze*, was made into a movie in 1996.
- **Catherine Lim** is one of Singapore's most successful novelists. She has written a number of novels, short stories and poems which focus on various aspects of Singaporean society.
- **Neil Humphreys** is not Singaporean (he's British by birth) but is one of the most beloved writers living in Singapore. He has written a number of books on Singapore society and other works of fiction.
- **Edwin Thumboo** is considered to be one of Singapore's literary pioneers. As many of his poems have nationalistic themes he is considered to be Singapore's unofficial poet laureate.
- **Cyril Wong** is a poet who is renowned for his candid poems. He has been a featured writer at many local and international writing festivals and has also edited many literary publications.

- **Alfian bin Sa'at** is a poet and playwright who writes in both Malay and English. He is renowned for his powerful and provocative works.

## Notorious
- **Annabel Chong** is Singapore's own international porn actress. Although now retired from the adult film industry she rose to prominence during the mid-1990s with her performance in *World's Biggest Gang Bang*.

## Online
- **Mr Brown** is the online persona of Lim Kin Mun and is one of Singapore's earliest online identities. His blog (mrbrown.com) began in 1997 and explores the 'dysfunctional side of Singapore life'.
- **Amos Yee** is a young man who, by voicing his opinions on various issues on social media, has wound up on the wrong side of Singapore's law.
- **Lady Iron Chef** is a food blogger, but don't be fooled by the name as the author is actually a man! His blog (www.ladyironchef.com) is a reliable source for food and travel reviews.
- **Xiaxue** is the online persona of Wendy Cheng. Although she initially started as a blogger on www.xiaxue.blogspot.com, she now posts across a wide variety of social media platforms and is known for her fashion, plastic surgery and parenting posts.

# ACRONYMS

Singapore is a city-state of acronyms. Just about every government department, board or corporation will abbreviate its name. Decoding the expressway acronyms used in a radio traffic report can take months! As well as the official translation of acronyms there are also commonly known humorous translations. The CPF (Central Provident Fund) which administers Singaporean's retirement funds is sometimes cheekily referred to as Coffin Provision Fund.

## Government Ministries

| | |
|---|---|
| MCI | Ministry of Communications and Information |
| MCCY | Ministry of Culture, Community and Youth |
| MINDEF | Ministry of Defence |
| MOE | Ministry of Education |
| MFA | Ministry of Foreign Affairs |
| MOH | Ministry of Health |
| MHA | Ministry of Home Affairs |
| MINLAW | Ministry of Law |
| MOM | Ministry of Manpower |
| MND | Ministry of National Development |
| MSF | Ministry of Social and Family Development |
| MEWR | Ministry of the Environment and Water Resources |
| MTI | Ministry of Transport |
| PMO | Prime Minister's Office |

## Government Agencies

| | |
|---|---|
| ACRA | Accounting and Corporate Regulatory Authority |
| A*STAR | Agency for Science Technology and Research |
| AVA | Agri-food and Veterinary Authority |
| BOA | Board of Architects |
| BCA | Building and Construction Authority |
| CRA | Casino Regulatory Authority of Singapore |
| CPF Board | Central Provident Fund Board |

| | |
|---|---|
| CAAS | Civil Aviation Authority of Singapore |
| CSC | Civil Service College |
| CCS | Competition Commission of Singapore |
| CEA | Council for Estate Agencies |
| CPE | Council for Private Education |
| DSTA | Defence Science and Technology Agency |
| EDB | Economic Development Board |
| EMA | Energy Market Authority |
| HPB | Health Promotion Board |
| HLB | Hotels Licensing Board |
| HDB | Housing & Development Board |
| IDA | Infocomm Development Authority of Singapore |
| IRAS | Inland Revenue Authority of Singapore |
| IPOS | Intellectual Property Office of Singapore |
| IE | International Enterprise Singapore |
| LTA | Land Transport Authority |
| MUIS | Majlis Ugama Islam, Singapura |
| MPA | Maritime and Port Authority of Singapore |
| MDA | Media Development Authority |
| MAS | Monetary Authority of Singapore |
| NAC | National Arts Council |
| NCSS | National Council of Social Services |
| NEA | National Environment Authority |
| NHB | National Heritage Board |
| NLB | National Library Board |
| NParks | National Parks Board |
| PA | People's Association |
| PDPC | Personal Data Protection Commission |
| PEB | Professional Engineer's Board, Singapore |
| PUB | PUB, The National Water Agency |

| PTC | Public Transport Council |
| SAF | Singapore Armed Forces |
| SBS | Singapore Bus Service |
| SCB | Science Centre Board |
| SAC | Singapore Accountancy Commission |
| SDC | Singapore Dental Council |
| SLA | Singapore Land Authority |
| SMC | Singapore Medical Council |
| SNB | Singapore Nursing Board |
| STB | Singapore Tourism Board |
| URA | Urban Redevelopment Authority |

## Other Bodies

| ACM | Asian Civilisations Museum |
| SAM | Singapore Arts Museum |
| NUS | National University of Singapore |
| NTUC | National Trades Union Congress |
| SDF | Skills Development Fund |
| FAS | Football Association of Singapore |
| CDAC | Chinese Development Assistance Council |
| SINDA | Singapore Indian Development Association |
| SLF | Singapore Labour Foundation |
| VWO | Voluntary Welfare Organisation |

## Political Parties

| PAP | People's Association Party |
| WP | Workers' Party |
| SDP | Singapore Democratic Party |
| SPP | Singapore People's Party |
| SDA | Singapore Democratic Alliance |
| NSP | National Solidarity Party |

## Banks

| | |
|---|---|
| DBS | Development Bank of Singapore |
| OCBC | Overseas Chinese Banking Corporation |
| OUB | Overseas Union Bank (now defunct, bought over by UOB—see below) |
| POSB | Post Office Savings Bank |
| UOB | United Overseas Bank |
| ANZ | Australia and New Zealand Banking Corporation |

## Hospitals

| | |
|---|---|
| AH | Alexandra Hospital |
| KK | Kandang Kerbau Women's and Children's Hospital |
| NUH | National University Hospital |
| SGH | Singapore General Hospital |
| TTSH | Tan Tock Seng Hospital |

## Transport

| | |
|---|---|
| AYE | Ayer Rajah Expressway |
| BKE | Bukit Timah Expressway |
| COE | Certificate of Entitlement |
| CTE | Central Expressway |
| ECP | East Coast Expressway |
| ERP | Electronic Road Pricing |
| IU | In-vehicle Unit |
| KJE | Kranji Expressway |
| KPE | Kallang–Paya Lebar Expressway |
| LRT | Light Rail Transport |
| MCE | Marina Coastal Expressway |
| MRT | Mass Rapid Transport |

| PIE | Pan Island Expressway |
| SLE | Seletar Expressway |
| TPE | Tampines Expressway |

## Miscellaneous

| LOC | Letter of Consent |
| TA | Tenancy Agreement |
| GST | Goods and Services Tax |
| NDP | National Day Parade |
| NS | National Service |
| PR | Permanent Resident |
| DP | Dependant Pass |
| EP | Employment Pass |
| NRIC | National Registration Identity Card |
| PSI | Pollution Standards Index |
| PEP | Personalised Employment Pass |
| SAM | Self-service Automated Machine |
| NETS | Network for Electronic Transfers Singapore |
| LOI | Letter of Intent |
| FDW | Foreign Domestic Worker |

# CULTURE QUIZ

## SITUATION 1

You arrive at a work meeting which you scheduled a couple of weeks in advance. There are four other people in the meeting: a male Chinese manager, a female *ang moh*, an Indian man, and a Malay lady. Should you shake everyone's hand?

**Ⓐ** Of course! That's how you introduce yourself at every meeting in your home country.

**Ⓑ** No, you shake the men's hands but kiss the women in the group on the cheek.

**Ⓒ** Wait and see how the members of the group introduce themselves. If they extend their hand then shake it. Otherwise smile and nod.

## Comments

The most appropriate answer is **C**. Some Muslim women (and the majority of Malay people are Muslim) are not comfortable shaking hands with members of the opposite sex, so it's always wise to follow the lead of the people you are meeting.

## SITUATION 2

Your next door neighbours are a lovely Chinese family, who you have become quite friendly with since you arrived. They invite you to their Chinese New Year dinner on the second day of Chinese New Year. What should you wear and what should you take?

**A** You decide to splash out and buy yourself new clothes to mark the occasion and opt for a festive red shirt. You take with you two mandarin oranges and some red packets with $2 notes inside to give to any children who may be attending.

**B** You stick to your usual style and dress all in black. As a gift for your host you take a bottle of wine.

**C** You wear some nice and presentable clothes from your wardrobe, but avoid white or black options. It doesn't occur to you to bring a gift.

## Comments

The most appropriate answer here is **A**. Amongst the Chinese community it's traditional to buy new clothes to celebrate CNY, but it's unlikely you will be asked to leave if you wear an outfit you already own! However, you should avoid wearing either white or black as these are both considered to be mourning colours. Red is the most festive choice, but other colours are also appropriate. Gift-giving is a large part of CNY celebrations and it is expected that guests will present the host with two mandarin oranges, which will be reciprocated when you leave. It would be considered rude to arrive empty-handed. You should also take some red packets with even number of dollars in them and hand these to any kids who are attending.

## SITUATION 3

You've noticed that in the last week or so that someone has been leaving cartons of food on the footpath as you walk from your condo to the MRT. There are also used joss sticks and a pile of ashes nearby. What do you do?

**A** Pick up the cartons of food and used joss sticks and place them in a nearby garbage can. Then, as you are very concerned about air pollution, call the National Environment Authority (NEA) to complain about the burning of the paper.

**B** Think to yourself that someone must have accidentally left their meal on the footpath and continue on your way.

**C** Think to yourself 'Ahhh....must be Hungry Ghost time!', leave everything as is and think to yourself how lucky you are to witness these cultural differences.

### Comments

The answer is **C**. The Hungry Ghost Festival is celebrated in the seventh month of the Chinese calendar. It is believed the gates of hell open and ghosts roam the earth for that month. In order to keep the spirits happy, food offerings are left for them and paper money is burnt. This is sometimes done at the front of people's homes on the footpath area and this shouldn't be disturbed. Just walk around the food, joss sticks and ashes and continue on your way.

## SITUATION 4

You take yourself and your family to Newton Hawker Centre for your first trip to a hawker centre. As you enter, you are greeted by a man holding a laminated menu and shown to a table. What do you do?

Ⓐ Take one look at the unfamiliar scene and head to the nearest McDonalds.

Ⓑ Reserve your table by placing a packet of tissues on the table and walk around the various stalls to see what they have to offer. You order dishes and drinks from a couple of different stalls and return to your choped table, not ordering from the man who seated you.

Ⓒ Bewildered by the experience, you order your entire meal from the man who seated you.

## Comments

The best answer here is **B** but, both **A** and **C** are quite normal reactions as your first trip to a hawker centre can be very daunting! 'Touting' is technically illegal in Singapore but there are some stallholders who by directing you to a table and presenting you with a menu imply that you must order from their stall. This isn't the case and in any food centre you are free to order from any stall. Just tell the man 'no, thank you' and he'll remove the menu and leave you alone with no hard feelings.

If everyone wants to walk around and look at the various stalls then it's acceptable to chope your table with a packet of tissues or an umbrella. You can order from as many stalls as you like and the dishes will be delivered to your table, unless the stall has a sign saying 'self-service'.

## SITUATION 5

After a long day of shopping on Orchard Road you decide to give yourself a treat by skipping the MRT in favour of a taxi. You chance upon a rather talkative taxi uncle who is very interested in your lifestyle. When you give him your address, he responds 'Wah! So expensive, lah! How much rent you pay?' How do you respond?

**A** Tell him that information is none of his business, thank you very much!

**B** Become a bit flustered and stutter out an explanation of how the company pays for your rent and that you have never lived anywhere as fancy as this before!

**C** Understand that the taxi uncle is just showing an interest in the way you live and give a ballpark figure. After all, the rental rates for your property can be Googled!

## Comments

The best answer here is definitely **⊙**, although I usually opt for **⊙**! The taxi uncle is not meaning to pry into your personal life and questions like these are simply a way of showing interest in someone. Give either a rough estimate or the exact figure and the taxi uncle will be happy. Whilst asking questions like this may not happen in your home culture you are better to just answer politely than getting angry or offended as there is no malice intended on the taxi uncle's behalf.

## SITUATION 6

You board a crowded MRT carriage with your young child. There are no vacant seats so you hold onto the pole. Although your child is happy to stand, a nearby lady offers her seat to your child. What do you do?

**⊙** Insist that you and your child are OK and refuse to take the seat.

**⊙** Gratefully say "thank you" and take the seat.

**⊙** Pretend you haven't heard to avoid making the wrong choice.

## Comments

Singaporeans adore children and almost every time I used the MRT when my children were under schoolgoing age, someone would offer them a seat. In the beginning I would try to refuse the offer but usually the person offering would remain standing, resulting in an awkward situation. I soon learnt that it was better to accept the seat and not offend the person offering it.

# DO'S AND DON'TS

## DO'S

- Remember that group harmony is more important than individual happiness.
- Be aware that seniority in either age or rank automatically earns respect and older or higher-ranked people should be treated with respect and courtesy at all times.
- Be mindful of the different cultures and religions. Whilst this can be a tricky balance, having a basic understanding of the beliefs and traditions of each of the three major ethnic groups helps to avoid major faux pas.
- Be considerate of how important 'face' is in Singaporean society. If you need to express disapproval to someone try to do this in a private setting so that they don't lose face.
- Point using either your whole hand or with a closed fist and your thumb extended.
- Remove your shoes before entering someone's home or a temple.
- Learn a few words of Singlish, Mandarin, Malay and Tamil. Whilst mastering new languages isn't needed to live in Singapore, learning a few basic words is a way of showing respect.
- Ask what the correct etiquette is if you are unsure. Singaporeans are more than happy to guide foreigners through the quirks of their culture.
- Throw yourself into the experience of living in a new country.

## DON'TS

- Don't criticise the government or make negative comments on religions or cultural traditions.

- Don't take offence at personal questions. This is a way of showing interest and not considered rude.

- Don't raise your voice or become aggressive. Singaporeans are very restrained in expressing their emotions and outbursts are generally frowned upon. You will get a better response by being calm and rational.

- Don't point the sole of your foot or shoe at anyone as they are considered unclean.

- When eating at a food centre, don't mix halal eating utensils with those from a non-halal stall.

- Don't use your left hand for moving food from your plate to your mouth or for giving gifts.

- Don't automatically shake hands with everyone as some groups of people are not comfortable with body contact. It's best to wait and follow their lead.

- Don't place chopsticks into a bowl such that they stand straight up as this indicates a food offering for the dead. Chopsticks should either be placed on a chopstick rest or laid together horizontally across the top of the bowl.

- Don't publically disagree with or correct superiors in public.

- Don't expect things to be the same as they were 'at home'. They won't be and that's half the fun of living in a new country!

# GLOSSARY

It's not necessary to learn a single word of a language other than English to live happily in Singapore. However, knowing a few basic words and phrases of the Mother Tongues is helpful and greatly appreciated by most Singaporeans.

| English | Malay | Mandarin | Tamil |
|---------|-------|----------|-------|
| Hello | Hello | *Ni hao* | *Vanakkam* |
| How are you? | *Apa khabar?* | *Ni hao ma?* | *Eppati irukkinga?* (or) *Nalamaa?* |
| Fine, thanks | *Baik, terima kasih* | *Hao, xiexie* | *Nalam or nalla irukkiren* |
| Thank you | *Terima kasih* | *Xie xie* | *Romba nandri* |
| Goodbye | *Selamat tinggal* | *Zai jian* | *Poi varuga,* or *poi varugiren* |
| Yes | *Ya* | *Shi* | *Aama* |
| No | *Tidak* | *Bu shi* | *Illai* |
| Please | *Tolong* | *Qing* | *Thayavu seithu* |
| One | *Satu* | *Yi* | *Ondru* |
| Two | *Dua* | *Er* | *Irandu* |
| Three | *Tiga* | *San* | *Moondru* |
| Four | *Empat* | *Si* | *Naanku* |
| Five | *Lima* | *Wu* | *Ainthu* |
| Six | *Enam* | *Liu* | *Aaru* |
| Seven | *Tujuh* | *Qi* | *Ezhu* |
| Eight | *Lapan* | *Ba* | *Ettu* |
| Nine | *Sembilan* | *Jiu* | *Onpathu* |
| Ten | *Sepuloh* | *Shi* | *Pathu* |

# RESOURCE GUIDE

Singapore uses eight-digit telephone numbers and as the island is small there are no area codes. A landline number begins with 6, while mobile phone numbers begin with either 8 or 9. There's no need to include the country code when calling local numbers within Singapore.

Toll-free numbers usually start with 1800, except for the emergency numbers.

## EMERGENCY NUMBERS

- **Police** — 999 (toll-free)
- **Emergencies/Ambulance/Fire** — 995 (toll-free)
- **Non-emergency ambulance** — 1777
- **Police hotline** — 1800 255 0000 (toll-free)
- **Traffic police** — 6547 0000

## USEFUL WEBSITES

- **ExpatSingapore** (www.expatsingapore.com)
  A great website for new expats to Singapore that covers a wide range of topics.
- **Expat Living Singapore** (www.expatliving.sg)
  This website also has a magazine and focuses on many different aspects of Singapore life.
- **Property Guru** (www.propertyguru.com.sg)
  This is a good website to search for rental properties but be warned that many of the listings are stock listings and the apartment or house you view may be different to what is listed online.
- **Go There** (www.gothere.sg)
  An incredibly useful transport website that guides you

from Point A to Point B by a variety of different forms of transport.

- **The Smart Local** (www.thesmartlocal.com)
  This website isn't targeted at expats, but that's a bonus as you'll learn lots of great information about the real Singapore.

## USEFUL APPS

- **Gothere.sg** – provides transport options and directions.
- **Grabtaxi** – a taxi booking app that covers all major taxi companies. There are also individual booking apps for all of the major taxi companies.
- **Mytransport.sg** – an app that keeps all land transport users (commuters, driver, and cyclists) up to date with current travel conditions and also helps them plan their trips.
- **WhereTo.sg** – locates the nearest services such as 7-11, supermarkets, ATMs, etc.
- **Hosay!** – a Singlish translation app that will help you understand and speak Singlish in no time, lah!

## HOSPITALS

- In the event of an emergency, you should head to a hospital. Any hospital will do as Singapore has excellent public hospitals. Full details of all hospitals and specialist centres can be found on the hospitals.sg website. The following list shows hospitals with **24-hour emergency departments**:

## Public Hospitals

- **Alexandra Hospital**
  378 Alexandra Road, 159964.
- **Changi General Hospital (CGH)**
  2 Simei Street 3, 529889.
- **Mount Alvernia Hospital**
  820 Thomson Rd, 574623.
- **National University Hospital (NUH)**
  5 Lower Kent Ridge Rd, 119074.
- **Singapore General Hospital (SGH)**
  Outram Rd, 169608.
- **Tan Tock Seng Hospital (TTSH)**
  11 Jalan Tan Tock Seng, 308433.
- **KK Women's and Children's Hospital (KKH)**
  100 Bukit Timah Road, 229899.
- **Ng Teng Fong General Hospital**
  1 Jurong East Street 21, 609606.

## Private Hospitals

- **Gleneagles Hospital**
  6A Napier Rd, 258500.
- **Mount Elizabeth Hospital Orchard**
  3 Mount Elizabeth, 228510.
- **Mount Elizabeth Hospital Novena**
  38 Irrawaddy Road, 329563
- **Raffles Hospital**
  585 North Bridge Rd, 188770.
- **Parkway East Hospital**
  321 Joo Chiat Place, 427990.
- **Thomson Medical Centre (TMC)**
  339 Thomson Rd, 307677.

# INTERNATIONAL SCHOOLS

- **Anglo-Chinese School (International)**
  www.acsinternational.com.sg
  61 Jalan Hitam Manis, 278475. Tel: 6472 1477

- **Australian International School Singapore**
  www.ais.com.sg
  1 Lorong Chuan, 556818. Tel: 6653 2958

- **Avondale Grammar School**
  www.avondale.edu.sg
  318 Tanglin Rd, Phoenix Park, 247979.
  Tel: 6258 8544

- **Canadian International School**
  www.cis.edu.sg
  Lakeside Campus: 7 Jurong West Street 41, 649414.
  Tel: 6467 1732
  Tanjong Katong Campus: 371 Tanjong Katong Road, 437128.
  Tel: 63451573

- **Chatsworth International School**
  www.chatsworth.com.sg
  Orchard Campus: 37 Emerald Hill Rd, 229313.
  Tel: 6737 5955
  East Campus: 25 Jalan Tembusu, 438234.
  Tel: 6344 5955

- **Dover Court International School**
  www.nordangliaeducation.com/our-schools/singapore
  301 Dover Road, 139644. Tel: 6775 7664

- **DPS International School**
  www.dps.com.sg
  36 Aroozoo Ave, 539842. Tel: 6285 6300

- **Dulwich College**
  www.dulwich-singapore.sg
  71 Bukit Batok West Avenue 8, 658966. Tel: 6890 1000

- **GEMS World Academy**
  www.gwa.edu.sg
  2 Yishun Street 42, 768039. Tel: 6808 7321
- **German European School Singapore**
  www.gess.sg
  72 Bukit Tinggi Rd, 289760. Tel: 6469 1131
- **Global Indian School Singapore**
  www.giissingapore.org
  Three campuses located at Queenstown, Balestier and East Coast. Main contact: 1 Mei Chin Road, 149253. Tel: 6508 3700
- **Hillside World Academy**
  www.hwa.edu.sg
  11 Hillside Drive, 548926. Tel: 6254 0200
- **Hollandse School**
  www.hollandseschool.org
  Bukit Tinggi Rd, 289757. Tel: 6466 0662
- **Hwa Chong International School**
  www.hcis.edu.sg
  663 Bukit Timah Road, 269783. Tel: 6464 7077
- **International Community School**
  www.ics.edu.sg
  27A Jubilee Rd, 128575. Tel: 6776 7435
- **International School Singapore**
  www.iss.edu.sg
  25 Paterson Road, 238510. Tel: 6235 5844
- **Lycée Français de Singapour**
  www.lfs.edu.sg
  3000 Ang Mo Kio Ave 3, 569928. Tel: 6488 1160
- **Nexus International School Singapore**
  www.nexus.edu.sg
  201 Ulu Pandan Rd, 596468. Tel: 6536 6566

- **NPS International School**
  www.npsinternational.com.sg
  10 Chai Chee Lane, 469021. Tel: 6294 2400
- **One World International School**
  www.owis.org
  696 Upper Changi Rd East, 486826. Tel: 6542 2285
- **Overseas Family School**
  www.ofs.edu.sg
  81 Pasir Ris Heights, 519292. Tel: 6738 0211
- **Singapore American School**
  www.sas.edu.sg
  40 Woodlands Street 41, 738547. Tel: 6363 3403
- **Singapore Korean International School**
  www.skis.kr
  71 Bukit Tinggi Rd, 289759. Tel: 6741 0778
- **Sir Manasseh Meyer International School**
  www.smm.edu.sg
  3 Jalan Ulu Sembawang, 758932.
  Tel: 6331 4633
- **St Joseph's Institution International School**
  www.sji.edu.sg
  490 Thomson Road, 298191. Tel: 6353 9383
- **Stamford American International School**
  www.sais.edu.sg
  1 Woodleigh Lane, 357684. Tel: 6602 7247
- **Swiss School**
  www.swiss-school.edu.sg
  38 Swiss Club Rd, 288140. Tel: 6468 2117
- **Tanglin Trust School**
  www.tts.edu.sg
  95 Portsdown Road, 139299. Tel: 6778 0771

- **The Japanese School Singapore**
  www.sjs.edu.sg
  201 West Coast Rd, 127383. Tel: 6779 7355
- **The Winstedt School**
  www.winstedt.edu.sg
  1208 Upper Boon Keng, 387312. Tel: 6715 5373
- **United World College**
  www.uwcsea.edu.sg
  Dover Campus: 1207 Dover Road, 139654.
  Tel: 6775 5344
  East Campus: 1 Tampines Street 73, 528704.
  Tel: 6305 5344
- **Yuvabharathi International School**
  www.yuvabharathi.sg
  3 Hu Ching Road, Jurong West, 619651.
  Tel: 6265 2342

## SOCIAL CLUBS AND ASSOCIATIONS

- **The American Club**
  www.amclub.org.sg
  10 Claymore Hill, 229573. Tel: 6737 3411
- **The British Club**
  www.britishclub.org.sg
  73 Bukit Tinggi Road, 289761. Tel: 6467 4311
- **Hollandse Club**
  www.hollandseclub.org.sg
  22 Camden Park, 299814. Tel: 6464 5225
- **The Swiss Club**
  www.swissclub.org.sg
  36 Swiss Club Rd, 288139. Tel: 6591 9420

- **The Japanese Association**
  www.jas.org.sg
  120 Adam Rd, 289899. Tel: 6591 8136
- **The Tanglin Club**
  www.tanglinclub.org.sg
  5 Stevens Rd, 257814. Tel: 6622 0555
- **Singapore Polo Club**
  www.singaporepoloclub.org
  80 Mt Pleasant Road, 298334. Tel: 6854 3999
- **German Association**
  61A Toh Tuck Road, 596300. Tel: 6467 8802
- **Singapore Cricket Club (SCC)**
  www.scc.org.sg
  Connaught Drive, 179681. Tel: 6338 9271
- **ANZA (Australian and New Zealand Association)**
  www.anza.org.sg
  47A Kampong Bahru Road, 169361. Tel: 6223 7992
- **American Women's Association (AWA)**
  www.awasingapore.org
  10 Claymore Hill, 229573. Tel: 6734 4895
- **Alliance Francaise**
  www.alliancefrancaise.org.sg
  1 Sarkies Road, 258130. Tel: 6737 8422
- **Canadian Association of Singapore**
  www.canadians.org.sg
  One Raffles Quay, Level 25, North Tower, 048583.
  Tel: 6622 5485
- **The British Association**
  www.britishassociation.org.sg
  19 Tanglin Rd, #03-61 Tanglin Shopping Centre,
  247909. Tel: 6339 8229

- **Korean Association**
  www.koreansingapore.org
  71b Tanjong Pagar Road, #03-01, 088492.
  Tel: 6299 8966
- **Spanish Speaking Women's Association**
  www.sswasingapur.com

## PLACES OF WORSHIP

There are many places of worship in Singapore and it would be almost impossible to include details of all of them here. For more details, refer to the various websites listed below.

- **The Anglican Diocese of Singapore**
  www.anglican.org.sg
- **Roman Catholic Archdiocese of Singapore**
  www.catholic.org.sg
- **The Methodist Church in Singapore**
  www.methodist.org.sg
- **The Presbyterian Church in Singapore**
  www.presbysing.org.sg
- **Lutheran Church in Singapore**
  www.lutheran.org.sg
- **International Baptist Church**
  www.ibcs.org
- **Armenian Church**
  www.armeniansinasia.org
- **The Church of Jesus Christ of Latter-Day Saints**
  www.mormon.org
- **The Assemblies of God Singapore**
  www.ag.org.sg
- **Buddhist and Chinese Temples**
  singapore-dharmanet.buddha.sg

- **Hindu temples**

  heb.org.sg
- **Islamic mosques**

  www.mosque.sg
- **Synagogues**

  www.singaporejews.org
- **Sikh temples**

  www.sikhs.org.sg
- **Jainism**

  www.sjrs.org.sg

# FURTHER READING

## HISTORY AND POLITICS

- *Crossroads: a popular history of Malaysia & Singapore*, Jim Baker, Marshall Cavendish, 2008.

  This general history of both Malaysia and Singapore explores the interdependence of the two countries in a balanced and critical manner.

- *The* Syonan *Years: Singapore under Japanese Rule 1942–1945*, Lee Geok Boi, National Archives of Singapore, 2005.

  This is a detailed recount of life in Singapore during the Japanese Occupation.

- *The Singapore* Story: *The Memoirs of Lee Kuan Yew*, Lee Kuan Yew, Marshall Cavendish, 2014.

  Lee Kuan Yew was not only the founding Father of Singapore but he is also a prolific author. In this book Mr Lee recounts how he helped transform Singapore from a fishing village to the modern city today.

- *Ousted!*, Patrick Keith, Media Masters, 2005.

  Most Singapore history books focus on the fifty years since Independence but this book solely explores the events surrounding the separation of Singapore from the Malay Federation in 1965.

## PEOPLE AND CULTURE

- *The Coxford Singlish Dictionary*, Colin Goh and Y.Y. Woo, 2009, Angsana Books.

  This is a good and extensive guide to all things Singlish.

- *Singapore at Random*, Editions Didier Millet, 2011
  A collection of random facts and stories on a wide range of Singaporean topics.
- *Sounds and Sins of Singlish and Other Nonsense*, Rex Shelley, 2009, Marshall Cavendish Editions.
  Another guide to Singlish.
- *50 Things to Love About Singapore*, Susan Long, ST Press, 2015.
  Published in 2015, this book features articles on a range of topics from Straits Times journalists.
- *Malay Weddings Don't Cost $50 and Other Facts About Malay Culture*, Hidayah Amin, Helang Books, 2014.
  This book covers not only Malay wedding traditions but also other Malay cultural traditions.
- *The Straits Chinese House: Domestic Life and Traditions*, Peter Lee and Jennifer Chen, National Museum of Singapore, 2006.
  This book is a look inside the house and cultural traditions of the Straits Chinese or Peranakan people.
- *Heritage Places of Singapore*, Wan Men Hao and Jacqueline Lau, Marshall Cavendish, 2009.
  This book features lots of different aspects of Singapore's heritage and includes gorgeous colour photos of each place.

## FOOD

- *There's* No *Carrot in Carrot Cake*, Ruth Wan and Roger Hiew, 2010, Epigram.

   This book features 101 common hawker dishes. It explains the ingredients of each dish, its origins, how to pronounce them, hawker market etiquette and includes a comprehensive guide to the main food courts and hawker markets. Highly recommended!

## CHILDREN'S BOOKS

- *Gateway to Singapore Culture: Celebrate Friendship, Harmony & Peace*, Rosemarie Somaiah and Zhuang Xinyan, 2013, Asiapac Books.

   This book is a good introduction for kids (and grown-ups!) to the different ethnicities and their traditions.

- *Sasha in Singapore*, Shamini Flint, 2005, Sunbear Publishing.

   This is a five-book series of picture books that feature an expat child exploring Singapore. There are also other books focussed on different parts of Asia.

- *Singapore Children's Favourite Storie*s, Di Taylor, 2003, Periplus.

   An illustrated collection of Singaporean stories, including the famous tiger under the billiard table at Raffles Hotel.

## FICTION AND MEMOIRS

- *Fistful of Colours*, Suchen Christine Lim, 1991.

   Winner of the 1992 Singapore Literature Prize, this novel takes place over a single day in the life of a young teacher, Ong Suwen.

- *If I Could Tell You*, Lee Jing Jing, Marshall Cavendish, 2012.

    As a HDB block is scheduled for redevelopment and its occupants leave one by one, their stories unfold, with a tragic twist in the last few days. This is an excellent novel about real Singaporeans that many expats may never encounter.

- *Diary of an Expat in Singapore*, Jennifer Gargiulo, Marshall Cavendish, 2013.

    A humorous take on some aspects of being an expat in Singapore, including lots of helpful information!

- *Kampong Spirit: Gotong Royong – Life In Potong Pasir, 1955–1965*, Josephine Chia, Marshall Cavendish, 2013.

    An interesting look into what life was like growing up in a kampong in early Singapore.

# ABOUT THE AUTHOR

**Kelly Jackson-Nash** relocated to Singapore from Melbourne, Australia, in May 2011 with her husband and two daughters. Although the job opportunity for her husband was the initial motivating factor for the move, the family saw the relocation as an adventure. Kelly has documented the ups-and-downs of expat life from the earliest planning days on her blog (www.ourbigexpatadventure.wordpress.com). Once the family were settled into life in Singapore, Kelly began to explore the Little Red Dot and particularly enjoyed exploring the lesser-known parts.

These adventures were often sparked by Kelly's lifelong love of history. A qualified secondary school History teacher, Kelly is currently completing two history degrees. Cemeteries and the stories they tell are one of her research interests and there is not a Singapore cemetery that she hasn't explored! *CultureShock! Singapore* is Kelly's first book.

# INDEX

Titles in the **CultureShock!** series:

| | | |
|---|---|---|
| Argentina | France | Philippines |
| Australia | Germany | Portugal |
| Austria | Great Britain | Russia |
| Bahrain | Greece | San Francisco |
| Bali | Hawaii | Saudi Arabia |
| Beijing | Hong Kong | Scotland |
| Belgium | Hungary | Sri Lanka |
| Berlin | India | Shanghai |
| Bolivia | Ireland | Singapore |
| Borneo | Italy | South Africa |
| Bulgaria | Jakarta | Spain |
| Brazil | Japan | Sri Lanka |
| Cambodia | Korea | Sweden |
| Canada | Laos | Switzerland |
| Chicago | London | Syria |
| Chile | Malaysia | Taiwan |
| China | Mauritius | Thailand |
| Costa Rica | Morocco | Tokyo |
| Cuba | Munich | Travel Safe |
| Czech Republic | Myanmar | Turkey |
| Denmark | Netherlands | United Arab Emirates |
| Dubai | New Zealand | USA |
| Ecuador | Norway | Vancouver |
| Egypt | Pakistan | Venezuela |
| Finland | Paris | Vietnam |

For more information about any of these titles, please contact the Publisher via email at: genref@sg.marshallcavendish.com or visit our website at: www.marshallcavendish.com/genref